"DAUGHTERS OF JEFFERSON, DAUGHTERS OF BOOTBLACKS"

There was in the address . . . a sentiment in reference to employment and certain names, such as "Sambo" and the gardener and the bootblack and the daughters of Jefferson and Washington. . . . I have asked what difference there is between the daughters of Jefferson and Washington and other daughters.

FREDERICK DOUGLASS
TO ELIZABETH CADY STANTON, 1869

"DAUGHTERS OF JEFFERSON, DAUGHTERS OF BOOTBLACKS"

Racism and American Feminism

by

BARBARA HILKERT ANDOLSEN

MERCER
UNIVERSITY PRESS

ISBN 0-86554-204-X (cloth)
ISBN 0-86554-205-8 (paper)

The paper used in this publication meets
the minimum requirements of American National Standard
for Information Sciences—Permanence of Paper
for Printed Library Materials, ANSI Z39.48-1984. ∞™

Library of Congress Cataloging-in-Publication Data
Andolsen, Barbara Hilkert.
    "Daughters of Jefferson, daughters of bootblacks."
    Includes bibliographies and index.
    1. Feminism—United States—History. 2. Women—
Suffrage—United States—History. 3. Afro-American
women—History. 4. Racism—United States—History.
5. United States—Race relations—History. I. Title.
HQ1426.A6827   1986   305.4'2'0973   86-816
ISBN 0-86554-204-X
ISBN 0-86554-205-8 (pbk.)

Contents

Acknowledgments

MY THANKS to staff members of the Schlesinger Library, Radcliffe College; Manuscript Division, Library of Congress; Manuscript Division, Mable I. King Library, University of Kentucky; Manuscript Division, Moorland-Spingarn Research Center, Howard University; and New York Public Library, Astor, Lenox and Tilden Foundations, who assisted me with competence and courtesy.

Members of the Consultation on Social Ethics in a Feminist Perspective, especially Beverly Wildung Harrison, Carol S. Robb, and Mary D. Pellauer, helped me sharpen sections of this work. I also appreciate the comments of Henry Bowden, Lorine M. Getz, and Emily Culpepper. I am grateful to Thomas Ogletree, Howard Harrod, and Peter Paris for their responses to an earlier version of this work. I thank Aquin O'Neill, Toni Craven, Eve Sokol, and Maria Louisa Martinez for essential assistance with child care.

I wish to thank the Ethel Mae Wilson Fund, Vanderbilt University, for support in the initial research stage. I also appreciate the support I received for the final, publication stage from the Research Council, Rutgers, The State University of New Jersey.

I am grateful to friends at both Vanderbilt University and Rutgers University who buoyed up my spirits throughout the course of this project.

My deepest gratitude goes to my son, Daniel, for his resourcefulness and independence, and to my daughter, Ruth, for her joyfulness. I do not have words appropriate to thank my husband, Alan, for his generous support.

Introduction

THIS BOOK is a work of feminist ethics written from a theological perspective. It probes racism as a moral challenge confronting the contemporary women's liberation movement. As a theological ethicist, I hope to contribute to the feminist struggle with racism by clarifying the position of white feminists as moral agents engaged in this struggle. In this book I highlight the moral fallibility of white feminists who suffer oppression insofar as we are women, but who are tempted to participate in the oppression of others insofar as we are beneficiaries of race and, perhaps, class privilege. The activities of America's first feminists—the suffragists of the nineteenth and early twentieth centuries—illuminate our current situation. If those of us who are white women have a realistic sense of our own capacity for evil—"sin," in theological language—then we will be better able to assess the impact of our actions on black persons and to understand more clearly what a commitment to the well-being of *all* women requires of us.[1]

Feminist ethics focuses on the experiences of women. It insists that the well-being of women must be central for any adequate notion of human well-being and the common good. It provides a critical analysis of attitudes, patterns of relationship, and social structures that diminish women on the basis of sex. Feminist ethics must have a complex mode of social analysis, for, as Judith Plaskow states, "we are becoming aware that race, class, and sex oppression are interstructured in the lives of many women. They interlock not in an additive way, so that one is oppressed as a woman and as black, for example, but in an integral way which alters the total experience of oppression."[2] Feminist ethics investigates the changes in attitudes and social structures that are necessary for all women (and men) to have the opportunity for full human development in mutually supportive communities. Feminist ethics emphasizes the value of relationships characterized by mutual respect, equality, and justice.

---

[1] I am a middle-class white woman. I have used the pronouns *we* and *us* in this book in order to stress that I am continuing to struggle with racism in my own attitudes and actions. The pronouns are in no way meant to suggest that I am not also addressing black women or any men who choose to read this book.

[2] Judith Plaskow, "Anti-Semitism: The Unacknowledged Racism," in *Women's Consciousness, Women's Conscience,* ed. Barbara Hilkert Andolsen, Christine E. Gudorf, and Mary D. Pellauer (Minneapolis: Winston/Seabury Press, 1985) 75.

Most contemporary white feminists deplore racial discrimination and white supremacy (the belief that whites are innately superior to blacks and should dominate society). Most white feminists see the women's movement as a movement to better the lives of *all* women. Some of us believe that to eradicate sexism would also be to eradicate racism. We like to think of ourselves as fighters against racism, not as persons infected with racism.

Many liberal[3] white feminists see racism primarily as a display of overt hostility toward, or an expression of innate superiority over, members of another racial group. But when women view racism primarily as individual and intentional acts of racial discrimination and hatred, they fail to recognize the complexity of racism in American society. Racism also includes collective action to construct and maintain social institutions that provide a disproportionate share of goods, benefits, and power to members of the white race. To participate without explicit dissent in economic, political, and cultural institutions that perpetuate racial privilege is to act to maintain the status quo.

Racism is a social reality that can best be seen not by focusing on the overt intentions of whites, but on the unfair advantages accruing to whites at the expense of blacks. All white women, including white feminists, have privileged positions *as white persons* in American society. All white women, including white feminists, participate in institutions that sustain that racial privilege. "All of us are born into an environment where racism exists. Racism affects all of our lives, but it is only white women who can 'afford' to remain oblivious to those effects."[4]

Because racism has a significant institutional component, all of us who are white participate in racism, no matter how pure our feelings toward women and men of color. In spite of our feminist commitment to justice for all in American society, those of us who are white feminists are not immune from the racism that pervades our society. White feminist racism is manifest in white feminist theories that pay little heed to the particular needs of black women and that describe the experience of privileged white women as if it were universal female experience. Those of us who are white feminists display racism when we select tactics to advance the cause of women without examining whether, in a racist society, those tactics will have unintended negative consequences for the black community. We also

---

[3]For a discussion of the word *liberal* as a term describing the political and economic philosophy of a large number of the supporters of the women's liberation movement, see Carol Robb, "The Impact of Feminism on Social Ethics," *Journal of Religious Ethics* (Spring 1981): 45-66, and the introduction to *Women's Consciousness, Women's Conscience*, ed. Andolsen, Gudorf, and Pellauer.

[4]Cherrie Moraga and Gloria Anzaldua, eds., *This Bridge Called My Back: Writings by Radical Women of Color* (Watertown MA: Persephone Press, 1981) 62.

manifest racism when we act within racist social structures to improve the situation of women without criticizing or challenging the racist impact of those institutions on black women.

This book focuses on the interstructuring of sexism and racism, with some attention to the intertwining of racism, sexism, and economic exploitation. Other forms of human oppression, including heterosexism, age discrimination, prejudice against those with various handicapping conditions, and cultural imperialism also intersect with racism and sexism. Multidimensional analyses that reflect the intertwining of more of these forms of oppression remain as a task for those dedicated to justice.

Historical experience separates white women from black women. Hispanic, Asian-American, and Native American women have unique experiences, too. It would be as inappropriate to lump the experiences of all these women together too readily under the label "experience of minority women" as it is for feminists to lump the experiences of white and black women together too quickly under the title "women's experience." In order to give serious attention to the historical particularities of women's experience, I have chosen to analyze the relationship between white feminists and black people. Similar analyses of the connections between white feminists and members of other disadvantaged ethnic groups are also needed.

The history of racism within the American feminist movement helps us to understand the magnitude of the moral challenge that faces contemporary white feminists as we struggle to overcome our own racism. To investigate this history is to learn that those of us who are white feminists, no matter how noble our original intentions, can claim no special moral power in the struggle against racism. In the late 1840s an early generation of white feminists began their struggle for women's rights with the avowed intention of promoting human rights for blacks as well as whites. Yet many white woman suffragists shared an ideology of white supremacy with the men they lived with and among and never held full social equality for blacks as a goal. By the end of the nineteenth century many white suffragists, functioning within a racist political system, found it to their own benefit to cooperate with racist social practices and to manipulate racist ideology.

Nineteenth-century white feminists were involved in a more subtle racism when they used the social myth of True Womanhood to bolster their demand for the ballot. These white feminists extolled the influence the virtuous, educated, cultivated homemaker and mother could wield if she possessed the vote. When white feminists used such images, tainted with class and race privilege, in an uncritical manner they were ignoring the experience of black women.

This book focuses first on aspects of the history of the woman suffrage movement—in particular, the works of three key white woman suffrage leaders: Elizabeth Cady Stanton, Anna Howard Shaw, and Carrie Chapman Catt.[5] Elizabeth Cady Stanton was the most original thinker among the founders of the nineteenth-century women's movement. As an author and orator she advocated both women's rights and the abolition of slavery. She was a moving force behind the Seneca Falls Convention of 1848—the first convention called in America solely to agitate for women's rights. During the Civil War Stanton helped found the Woman's National Loyal League, which pressured Congress to emancipate the slaves as a war measure. In 1869 she was a founder of the National Woman Suffrage Association (NWSA). Stanton was a major theorist for the woman suffrage movement and served as president of the NWSA for 21 years, until it merged with the American Woman Suffrage Association. Later, she was president of the successor National American Woman Suffrage Association (NAWSA) for two more years.

A new generation began to assume key national posts in the suffrage movement by 1890. Among the intellectually gifted leaders of this later period were Carrie Lane Chapman Catt and Anna Howard Shaw. Between 1900 and 1920 they were the only presidents of NAWSA. Catt was a clever and logical speaker, but her greatest contribution to the movement was her organizational genius. Her direction of the campaign that gained ratification for the Nineteenth Amendment in a period of fourteen months was her tour de force. Anna Howard Shaw was an ordained minister in the Methodist Protestant Church. In a period when public speaking had far more influence in the shaping of public opinion, Shaw was the most famous orator of the women's movement.

Black suffragists challenged racism within the woman suffrage movement; among the more eloquent were Anna Julia Cooper and Mary Church Terrell.[6] Anna Julia Cooper was born a slave in North Carolina. A career educator, she described her views as a Southern black feminist in her collected essays, A Voice from the South. Mary Church Terrell was a lecturer and women's club leader who worked on behalf of black rights.

---

[5]Some of the best sources of additional information about the lives of these women are: Elizabeth Cady Stanton, *Eighty Years and More: Reminiscences, 1815-1897,* ed. Gail Parker (New York: Schocken Books, 1971); Theodore Stanton and Harriot Stanton Blatch, eds., *Elizabeth Cady Stanton as Revealed in Her Letters, Diary and Reminiscences* (New York: Harper and Brothers, 1922); Elisabeth Griffith, *In Her Own Right: The Life of Elizabeth Cady Stanton* (New York: Oxford University Press, 1984); Mary Gray Peck, *Carrie Chapman Catt: A Biography* (New York: H. W. Wilson Co., 1944); Anna Howard Shaw, *The Story of a Pioneer* (New York: Harper and Brothers, 1915).

[6]See Mary Church Terrell, *A Colored Woman in a White World* (Washington: Ransdell, 1940); and Louise Daniel Hutchinson, *Anna J. Cooper, A Voice from the South* (Washington: Smithsonian Institution Press, 1981).

She was also active in the woman suffrage movement and addressed both national and international women's meetings.

The history of the woman suffrage movement highlights the morally vulnerable social location of contemporary white feminists. We suffer disadvantage on the basis of our sex, but we also draw social benefit from our membership in a privileged race. As feminists, we have a moral obligation to inform ourselves about the distinctive situations confronting black women and to seek out and respect the distinctive social vision of black feminists.

We should take the initiative to inform ourselves about the views of black feminists who are creating a growing body of material describing women's liberation from a black vantage point. We need to study seriously the experiences of black women. Black feminists rightly complain that their energies are drained by constant demands to explain their lives to white feminists. It is not "the responsibility of the oppressed to teach the oppressors their mistakes."[7] In order to be partners in a dialogue about issues that affect all women, white feminists need to learn about the perspectives of black women without placing extra burdens on black feminists. One technique is to study literature by black women (fiction and nonfiction).

Black writers stress that their social experience is not identical to that of white women. As a result, their analyses of social conditions and assignment of priorities for the liberation of women differ from those of white feminists. Black feminist perspectives on rape, work (especially domestic work), female/male solidarity, and female beauty demonstrate these differences. White feminists have a responsibility to seek out such analyses, to study them sympathetically, and to shape our ideas and actions in light of these challenges.

Overconfidence about our moral strength as white feminists will impede the process of confronting our involvement in racism. Some white feminist theologians have renewed a form of the True Womanhood myth by extolling the moral strengths of women. Such an overemphasis on women's moral strength makes it difficult for white feminists to acknowledge our participation in racism and to admit the difficulty of rooting out that racism.

The temptation facing white feminist theologians is to describe our own experience as if it were universal female experience, obscuring both the special insights of black women and the moral fallibility of white women. We must not employ simplistic models of social evil. An adequate feminist social ethic must include an analysis of the *interstructuring* of racism, sexism, and economic exploitation. Unless black women (a disproportionate

---

[7]Audre Lorde, *Sister Outsider: Essays and Speeches* (Trumansburg NY: Crossing Press, 1984) 114.

number of whom are poor) can satisfy their material needs and can participate in economic decision making, many of the new rights exercised by more privileged women will remain hollow promises for them.

For white women to achieve greater human fulfillment, we must press for full recognition of our own human dignity while also struggling to create a system that fosters human wholeness for all women—and ultimately all persons. Those of us who are white women are diminished by sinful, distorted relationships between the races. A social system that denies freedom and wholeness to some persons diminishes all of us.

In order to persist in the struggle for social transformation, feminists need the support and challenge of communities of accountability—groups in which persons from diverse racial, ethnic, and economic backgrounds hold themselves mutually responsible for the struggle to create a more just society. At present, for many white feminists, participation in such communities is a difficult, fragmentary, and tenuous experience. But we require such experiences in order to orient and sustain us in the struggle for more just relationships and social structures. We need the humility and realism learned through listening to black women speak. We must hold ourselves accountable to black women for both our social vision and our actions.

1 | The Woman Suffrage Movement and the Black Freedom Movement

MANY EARLY FEMINISTS began their careers as women's rights activists in response to barriers they had encountered *as women* in the struggle to win freedom for black slaves. Nineteenth-century feminists played such a major role in the antislavery struggle that Frederick Douglass declared, "the cause of the slave has been peculiarly woman's cause."[1] But alliances between women's rights leaders and other abolitionists were severely strained when the rights of black freedmen and the rights of women were pitted against each other in the period immediately following black emancipation.

Feminists faced a sharp conflict of interest over ratification of the Fourteenth Amendment, which protected Negro suffrage but was a stumbling block to woman suffrage. Some white feminists broke off close relationships with blacks during this period. They separated their claims for justice from the claims being voiced by black people. White women began instead to tolerate passively or to manipulate actively racist attitudes as a means to obtain woman suffrage.

Early Solidarity

In the early days of the woman suffrage movement its white leaders saw their struggle as part of a larger struggle for human freedom. They fought for liberty for black people at the same time that they struggled for greater legal rights for themselves. Their rhetoric stressed universal human rights. The early career of Elizabeth Cady Stanton is representative of the commitment to both black rights and women's rights that characterized the feminists of this early period.

Stanton's shift from a radical abolitionist stance to staunch support for educated suffrage illustrates the dominant movement within the woman suffrage movement on the race question, that is, from basic egalitarianism to overt Anglo-Saxon noblesse oblige. There were, of course, supporters of woman suffrage who fought such a shift. Frederick Douglass, Mary Church Terrell, William Lloyd Garrison, Jr., Alice Blackwell, Ida B. Wells-Barnett, and others criticized racism within the movement. But it was

---

[1]Philip S. Foner, ed., *Frederick Douglass on Women's Rights* (Westport CT: Greenwood Press, 1976) 103.

women like Stanton, who accepted and acted upon the racist spirit of the times, who prevailed.

Stanton discovered her own oppression, in part, by watching women hampered by sex role restrictions in their attempts to help blacks. Indeed, it was within the abolitionist struggle that Stanton committed herself to challenge women's social and political deprivation. Stanton claimed that she formed the intention to agitate for women's rights as a result of her experiences as an observer at the 1840 World's Anti-Slavery Convention held in London. American abolitionist societies had elected several prominent women as members of their delegation. The British, who had never anticipated such unseemly female assertiveness, refused to accept the women's credentials, touching off a full day's debate on woman's proper role in social reforms. Finally, male delegates refused to seat the women and requested that they remain in a curtained gallery from which they could modestly listen to the male discussion. Several American male delegates refused to take their seats in protest against the convention's decision. Among these men was Charles Lenox Remond, a black leader who chose instead to join the exiled women in the gallery. Stanton, while not herself a delegate, was indignant at the treatment the women received. Along with Lucretia Mott, Stanton resolved to call a conference to protest the social restrictions suffered by women. In 1848 this resolve was fulfilled with the calling of the Seneca Falls Convention, the first public meeting to agitate for women's rights ever held in America.

The women who attended the convention were joined by the black orator, Frederick Douglass. Earlier, Douglass had been inclined by custom to object to arguments for women's rights. But in private conversation with Stanton her pleas for justice for women had overcome his objections and converted him to women's rights. So when Stanton introduced a controversial resolution demanding the ballot for women, Douglass spoke in its support. Although even Lucretia Mott considered the suffrage resolution too daring, it passed by a narrow margin, in part because of Douglass's support. Soon thereafter Douglass, who edited a paper called the *North Star,* published one of the few sympathetic editorials to appear in response to the historic Seneca Falls meeting.[2]

From 1848 to 1861, though hampered by heavy family responsibilities, Stanton wrote and spoke on behalf of both women's rights and abolitionism. A forceful example of her work is a pamphlet on behalf of free speech for abolitionists. She condemned the use of mob violence to disrupt antislavery meetings and reminded apathetic Americans that by safeguarding free speech for unpopular abolitionists they also safe-

---

[2]"The Rights of Women," *The North Star,* 28 July 1848, reprinted in Elizabeth Cady Stanton, Susan B. Anthony, and Mathilda J. Gage, eds., *The History of Woman Suffrage* (New York: Fowler and Wells, 1881) 1:74-75.

guarded their own right to free speech.[3] Throughout her career Stanton continued to assert that as long as the rights of social outcasts could be denied arbitrarily, the rights of all were precariously held.

Stanton's interest in the suffering of slaves was of long standing. As a young woman she had been deeply moved by the plight of a slave girl she had encountered in the home of her cousin, the prominent philanthropist and reform leader Gerrit Smith, whose home was a stop on the underground railroad. During her youth Stanton was also touched by the misery of married women who were legal clients of her father. Some of those women had been deprived of property and even child custody by cruel or drunken husbands. Stanton used these youthful memories when she drew an analogy between the plight of slaves and married women.

> The Negro has no name. He is Cuffy Douglass or Cuffy Brooks, just whose Cuffy he may chance to be. The Woman has no name. She is Mrs. Richard Roe or Mrs. John Doe, just whose Mrs. she may chance to be. Cuffy has no right to his earnings; he cannot buy or sell, or lay up. Mrs. Roe has no right to her earnings; she can neither buy or sell, make contracts, nor lay up anything that she can call her own. Cuffy has no right to his children; they can be sold from him at any time. Mrs. Roe has no right to her children; they may be bound out to cancel a father's debt of honor. The unborn child, even by the last will of the father, may be placed under the guardianship of a stranger and a foreigner. Cuffy has no legal existence; he is subject to restraint and moderate chastisement. Mrs. Roe has no legal existence; she has not the best right to her own person. The husband has the power to restrain, and administer moderate chastisement.[4]

Analogies between woman's experience and slave experience are sprinkled throughout the writings of early nineteenth-century feminists. In a piece in *The Revolution,* Stanton contended that the laws governing married women in 1868 were as unjust as the slave codes of the Old South. In an editorial two months later she portrayed the parallel suffering of white women and black people. Neither blacks nor white women had a voice in government. Both groups heard the Bible quoted to justify their subjection to white male masters. Both were denied access to professional training and practice. Both were used as objects to satisfy the white man's evil urges: black people were used to satisfy his avarice; women, his lust.[5]

---

[3]Elizabeth Cady Stanton, *Free Speech* (n.p., 1861).

[4]Stanton, Anthony, and Gage, eds., *History of Woman Suffrage*, 1:680-81.

[5]"The Degradation of Woman," *The Revolution*, 15 January 1868, 25-26; "Man the Usurper," *The Revolution*, 12 March 1868, 152.

Stanton failed, however, to observe that *black slave women* were used *both* as forced laborers and as sex objects by white masters.

As late as 1891 Stanton was still comparing the situation of white women and blacks. She indicated that cultivated black people, such as Robert Purvis, felt keenly the social insults offered them as a result of race. In similar fashion, white women felt keenly the insult offered them by society's refusal to acknowledge their full citizenship by granting them the franchise.

> We cannot make men see that women feel the humiliation of these petty distinctions of sex precisely as the black man feels those of color. It is no palliation of our wrongs to say that we are not socially ostracised as he is, so long as we are politically ostracised as he is not.[6]

The culmination of Stanton's dedication to universal human rights was her 1867 address to the New York state legislature. The legislature was planning a state constitutional convention. Stanton sought to have the constitution amended to enfranchise all women and poor black men. (New York law enfranchised all white men, but required that black men meet a $250 property qualification.) As a first step Stanton asked legislators to give women and black men a vote in the election of convention delegates.

Stanton theorized that during a constitutional convention the existing constitution is, in effect, suspended. Society returns in a sense to that state of nature wherein adults mutually pledge themselves to form a just government. The consent of all adults in the society is required. That consent must be obtained through representatives—the convention delegates—who should be selected by a vote of all adult citizens, including poor black men and all women. Since black men and all women compose a majority of the adult population, any government constituted without their consent would be a tyranny of the white male minority.

Stanton advocated that the suffrage be distributed as broadly as possible. The state has to justify exclusion of any citizen from the voter list. In particular, the state has to show that such exclusions do not fall disproportionately on natural subgroups within the society. Thus, exclusions based on race and sex are manifestly unjust. "As to color and sex . . . such insurmountable qualifications, not to be tolerated in a Republican gov-

---

[6]"The Degradation of Disfranchisement," Elizabeth Cady Stanton Papers, box 10, Library of Congress, Washington DC. On this occasion Stanton compared herself explicitly to the black man Robert Purvis. Stanton's admiration for well-educated, refined black men and women suggests that her racism was strongly rooted in class distinctions. She resented the fact that men who were beneath her in education and character had the vote, while she did not.

ernment, are unworthy of our serious consideration."[7] By contrast, age requirements are acceptable, for the maturity of judgment necessary to exercise the franchise is reasonably related to age. Age qualifications also affect all persons equally. All persons are disqualified for a set period, and all persons surviving into adulthood then gain an equal vote.

Age is an acceptable voter qualification; race and sex are not. That left two other common qualifying factors—property and education. Stanton gave these two careful consideration, but ultimately rejected both on grounds which showed a great respect for black people. Property and educational qualifications seem equitable. Conceivably, all persons can gain a basic education or amass a modest amount of personal property. But such qualifications set up the state as the judge of the worth of its citizens. Stanton insisted that power flows not from the state to worthy citizens, but from all the governed to the government. "A limited suffrage creates a privileged class, and is based on the false idea that government is the natural arbiter of its citizens, while in fact it is the creature of their will."[8] Showing respect for the poor and the illiterate, Stanton asserted that wisdom and virtue do not necessarily go hand in hand with wealth and education. She reminded the legislators that poor, illiterate black men had served with distinction during the Civil War, while wealthy, well-educated men had paid others to serve in their place. She also recalled that Jesus and his disciples lacked wealth and education. At this point in the Reconstruction period, Stanton still held a vision of all women marching through the gate of suffrage on the arm of uniformed black veterans.

Conflicting Interests

The Impact of the Fourteenth Amendment

As Reconstruction went forward, supporters of universal suffrage faced a crisis. The Fourteenth Amendment to the federal constitution was drafted to deal with a variety of legal problems that arose following the Civil War. Among these problems was a constitutional provision to count each slave as three-fifths of a person for the purpose of apportioning representation in the House of Representatives. After the emancipation of the slaves, a provision was drafted for the Fourteenth Amendment stipulating that all persons (except untaxed Indians) were to be counted equally. In an effort to safeguard the political rights of black men it also cut the representation of states that denied any male citizen the right to vote.

---

[7]Elizabeth Cady Stanton, *Address in Favor of Universal Suffrage, for the Election of Delegates to the Constitutional Convention* (Albany: Weed, Parsons and Company, 1867) 19-20.

[8]Ibid., 20.

But when the right to vote . . . is denied to any of the *male* inhabitants of such State, being twenty-one years of age, and citizens of the United States, or in any way abridged, . . . the basis of representation therein shall be reduced in the proportion which the number of such *male* citizens shall bear to the whole number of *male* citizens twenty-one years of age in such State.[9]

Prior to the ratification of the Fourteenth Amendment, the Constitution nowhere expressly connected maleness and the franchise.

While suffragists supported the aims of the Fourteenth Amendment, they opposed the language of this section, which used "male" as an adjective describing "citizen" in a context connected with voting. They made an attempt to have the offending word expunged from the draft of the amendment so that they could give it their unqualified support. However, a key congressional leader sympathetic to women's rights, Charles Sumner, reported that any draft of the amendment that was ambiguous on the question of woman suffrage would not get the full support of the Republican party, which dominated Congress in the period immediately after the Civil War.[10] Any wording other than "male citizen" jeopardized the votes needed to ensure congressional passage of the amendment.

Reformers who supported universal suffrage were caught on the horns of a dilemma. If they acted to help black men, they hurt women, and vice versa. Elizabeth Cady Stanton and others rightly predicted that passage of the Fourteenth Amendment would force women to seek another amendment to the federal constitution in order to guarantee woman suffrage. Since amending the Constitution is a laborious process, the success of the Fourteenth Amendment meant much additional work for advocates of woman suffrage.

Two years later Republicans drafted the Fifteenth Amendment, which expressly prohibited denial of the vote on the basis of race, color, or previous condition of servitude. This time woman suffrage advocates attempted to get the legislators to include sex as an improper ground for denial of the vote. Again white male politicians replied that to link black male suffrage with woman suffrage would only jeopardize the former.

While the Fourteenth and Fifteenth Amendments were detrimental to woman suffrage, they offered an important benefit to black men and potentially to black women. Given the political dominance of the Republican party following the Civil War, there was an excellent chance that Republican leaders could force adoption of the amendments protecting black men's rights. Black women stood to benefit from these amendments as well.

---

[9]United States Constitution, Amendment XIV, sec. 2. Emphasis added.

[10]Elizabeth Cady Stanton, Susan B. Anthony, and Mathilda J. Gage, eds., *The History of Woman Suffrage* (New York: Fowler and Wells, 1882) 2:91.

The Fourteenth Amendment protected their civil rights in general, if not their unrecognized right to vote. The amendments also offered the black race some access to the polls. Thus, black men, at least, would have the same means to protect the interests of black women that white men had to protect the interests of white women.

The proposal of the Fourteenth Amendment, which protected the voting rights of black men but explicitly excluded women, led white women to reevaluate their relationship with the black freedom movement. At this point, the drive for black men's rights was in conflict with, not parallel to, the drive for women's rights. The basic issue for woman suffrage leaders took the form of a question about conflicting interests. Did concern for black people entail that white women must set aside their own claims in order to help black men take advantage of the political opportunity open to them? Or could white women legitimately pursue their own self-interest regardless of the effects of their actions on the political fortunes of black men?

Debating Priorities

The conventions of the American Equal Rights Association, which had been formed by women's rights leaders to press for universal suffrage, became an important arena in which white women, black women, and black men asserted their conflicting interests. At the first annual meeting in 1867 Elizabeth Cady Stanton was asked directly whether she opposed Negro suffrage in the event that it should be obtained before woman suffrage. She replied,

> I would not trust him [the black man] with my rights; degraded, oppressed himself, he would be more despotic than even our Saxon rulers are. I desire that we go into the kingdom together; for individual and national safety demand that not another man be enfranchised without the woman by his side.[11]

This quote aptly summarizes Stanton's position in the late 1860s. She genuinely supported universal suffrage. However, if only some from among the disfranchised were to be given the ballot, she advocated woman suffrage.

She gave three reasons for her position. First, as a woman, woman suffrage was in her own direct interest. Stanton believed that self-preservation was one of the strongest natural instincts. Thus, it was only natural for white women to assert their own claims in a situation of conflict. Second, Stanton thought that women had innate personality characteristics different from those of men. Women had an inborn moral sensibility that was sorely needed in government. If only one group could be enfran-

---

[11]*Proceedings of the First Anniversary of the American Equal Rights Association* (New York: Robert J. Johnston, 1867) 53.

chised, that group should be women who would contribute a badly needed fresh perspective on social conditions. Third, Stanton viewed the vast majority of black men as ignorant and degraded. If they got the vote before women, they would oppose legislation benefiting women even more vigorously than did white men. As political superiors, black men would be more tyrannical toward white women than were white men with whom white women shared ties of culture and affection.

Stanton did not offer evidence to document her claim that black men would be more tyrannical than Anglo-Saxon men. Indeed, such an assertion would have been hard to support, for the evidence was mixed. Black feminists Sojourner Truth and Frances Ellen Watkins Harper did criticize some black freedmen for exercising a harsh dominance over freedwomen. Those white women who were aiding the freed slaves also uniformly criticized newly freed males for attempting to assert patriarchal dominance within the family. However, historian Jacqueline Jones suggests that the situation in newly freed families was complex and defied "simple categorization based on a vague standard of gender equality."[12]

Yet, while black male reformers, politicians, and labor leaders did not treat black women as full equals, their attitudes towards women's rights were frequently more progressive than those of their white counterparts. Antebellum black male leaders sometimes resisted giving black women decision-making power. Nevertheless, they were more willing to accept women as coworkers and were more supportive of women's rights than were white male reformers. In the period immediately after the Civil War black male politicians and labor leaders again supported women's rights more vigorously than did many of their white counterparts.[13] While some black men succumbed to the lures of patriarchal dominance, it was far from clear that black men were worse than—or even as bad as—white men.

Stanton's priority for woman suffrage was challenged by Abby Kelley Foster, a distinguished white abolitionist orator. She reported that whites were committing atrocities against black people in former slave states. Asserting that it was imperative that black men be offered full civil rights immediately as a means of self-protection, she asked, "are we not dead to the

---

[12]Stanton, Anthony, and Gage, eds., *History of Woman Suffrage*, 2:193; Paula Giddings, *When and Where I Enter: The Impact of Black Women on Race and Sex in America* (New York: William Morrow and Company, 1984) 64; Jacqueline Jones, "Freed Women? Black Women, Work and the Family During the Civil War and Reconstruction," p. 57, Working Paper #61, Wellesley College Center for Research on Women, Wellesley MA.

[13]Rosalyn Terborg-Penn, "Black Male Perspectives on the Nineteenth-Century Woman," in *The Afro-American Woman: Struggles and Images*, ed. Sharon Harley and Rosalyn Terborg-Penn (Port Washington NY: Kennikat Press, 1978) 28-42; Giddings, *When and Where I Enter*, 68-70.

sentiment of humanity if we shall wish to postpone his security against present woes and future enslavement till woman shall obtain political rights?"[14]

Parker Pillsbury, coeditor of *The Revolution,* defended Stanton, retorting that she did not "believe in loving her neighbor better than herself."[15] He contended that Stanton only asked for herself what she was willing to ask for others—immediate enfranchisement. She was fully willing to press the demands of black men, but not at the expense of her own rights.

At the next annual meeting of the American Equal Rights Association, Frederick Douglass urged support for Negro suffrage. He argued, as Abby Kelley Foster had the previous year, that Negroes were in extreme danger and thus had the more urgent need for the suffrage. He pointed to terrorist activities by the Ku Klux Klan and the Regulators. Douglass also chided Stanton and Anthony for accepting support from the eccentric Democrat George Francis Train. Train was a flamboyant politician known in part for his anti-Negro views. In Kansas, stumping for woman suffrage, Train had bluntly declared, "Woman first, and negro last, is my programme; yet I am willing that intelligence should be the test."[16]

In 1869 the American Equal Rights Association had a prolonged debate on the issue that had been troubling it for three years—should Negro (male) suffrage be given a tactical priority?[17] Stephen Foster objected to Stanton as president of the group because of her association with Train and because her paper, *The Revolution,* supported educated suffrage. A supporter of Stanton replied that Train was no longer providing financial backing for *The Revolution,* and thus Stanton had no further connection to the man. Stanton proceeded to give a speech in which she objected to ill-educated, lower-class men getting the vote before well-educated, white women. Douglass immediately objected to the upper-class prejudices that Stanton had expressed. Susan B. Anthony stood by Stanton, contending that if the country were to resort to granting partial suffrage, intelligent women should be the ones to get the vote.

---

[14]*Proceedings of the American Equal Rights Association,* 55.

[15]Ibid., 61.

[16]Stanton, Anthony, and Gage, eds., *History of Woman Suffrage,* 2:245. I was unable to find any direct response to Douglass's criticism of Stanton's and Anthony's association with Train. However, on a similar occasion Stanton justified her association with Train by stating, "your test of faithfulness is the negro, ours is the woman; the broadest platform, to which no party has yet risen, is humanity." Ibid., 264.

[17]Excerpts from the debates during the 1869 meeting of the American Equal Rights Association are found in Stanton, Anthony, and Gage, eds., *History of Woman Suffrage,* 2:378-99.

Frederick Douglass proposed a resolution hailing the extension of suffrage to black men as "a cheering part of the triumph of our whole idea" and urging passage of the Fifteenth Amendment as a further guarantee of black civil rights. A white law student, Phoebe Couzins, rose to protest that black women's rights were not recognized under the Fifteenth Amendment. Black women suffered all the legal disabilities of white women. Their lack of legal rights was especially serious since black men brutalized by slavery were using physical violence against women within their newly freed families. White activist Paulina Wright Davis said that she would support passage of the Fifteenth Amendment only if a sixteenth amendment granting equal rights to women were passed at the same time. She too was concerned about the plight of black women subjugated by black men. "Take any class that have been slaves and you will find that they are the worst when free and become the hardest masters." Douglass acknowledged that some black slaves were tyrants when they were made overseers by their white masters. Under scrutiny by the master, drivers had to demonstrate that they showed no favoritism to other slaves. It was white manipulation that provoked slave cruelty; now that blacks were free, brutality toward other blacks was no problem.[18]

Black writer Frances Ellen Watkins Harper asked whether Stanton and Anthony meant to include black women in the drive for woman suffrage. Anthony assured her that they did. Nonetheless, Harper declared, "If the nation could only handle one question she would not have the black woman put a single straw in the way, if only the men of the race could obtain what they wanted."[19]

White delegate Mary Livermore, voicing the impatience of others with the prolonged debate, moved the previous question. Douglass's resolutions were defeated.

Women's Rights as White Women's Priority

Founding the NWSA

At the close of the American Equal Rights Association meeting in 1869 a group of women dedicated to women's rights as their first priority met at the Woman's Bureau. They formed a new organization, the National Woman Suffrage Association (NWSA), dedicated solely to securing the franchise for women. While personal animosities among advocates of woman suffrage played a part in the decision to form the new organization, the founders were also unwilling to continue to debate the importance of woman suffrage with women and men who gave black male

[18]Foner, ed., *Frederick Douglass on Women's Rights,* 44; Stanton, Anthony, and Gage, eds., *History of Woman Suffrage,* 2:387, 391.

[19]Ibid., 2:392.

suffrage a higher priority. The editors of the *History of Woman Suffrage* explained, "The constant conflict on the Equal Rights platform proved the futility of any attempt to discuss the wrongs of different classes in one association."[20]

Thus Stanton and her allies turned their backs on an organization, the American Equal Rights Association, in which all—women and men, whites and blacks—were vigorously called to account for the effects of their policies and priorities on various disadvantaged social groups. Black men and women continued to be members and guests of the NWSA, but they never again had the freedom to speak publicly as full partners in a universal struggle for human rights. Their statements criticizing the actions and statements of white suffragists were voices from the fringe of the NWSA and its successor organization.

Once black people and white women had quarreled over priorities, Stanton no longer treated black rights and women's rights as necessarily linked. Instead she concentrated her energies on gaining women's rights. In the years that followed, she made only brief parenthetical pleas for black rights. Typical was an aside to the Judiciary Committee: "In the settlement, then, of what we choose to call the race problem, let us do justice and protect the freedman in his civil and political rights."[21] Stanton continued by saying that while she had departed from her planned remarks in making that statement, her comments were just an extension of her major point that all persons should be self-governing. Though black men still aroused Stanton's concern, no longer was she appealing to legislators primarily for recognition of the common claim of black men and all women to the ballot. Now black men's rights were clearly of secondary importance to Stanton.

Once Stanton became convinced that universal suffrage for women and black men was not readily attainable, she exhorted women to devote themselves to their own cause. "If you are a slave, it is your business to break the yoke that galls your own neck; you are to accept slavery or degradation at no price, from no mistaken notions of white men's rights or black men's wrongs."[22]

Cooperating with Racism

After 1890 a new generation of suffrage leaders began to assume key posts in the movement. Too young to have taken any active role in the antislavery struggle, they had no personal experience linking their own oppression as white women with the oppression of blacks. Thus, it was rel-

---

[20]Ibid., 2:400.

[21]Clipping, 1884 Presidential Address by Elizabeth Cady Stanton, Susan B. Anthony Collection, Rare Book Collection, Library of Congress, Washington DC.

[22]Elizabeth Cady Stanton, "Sharp Points," *The Revolution*, 9 April 1868, 212.

atively easy for them to press for their own interests independent of the interests of blacks.

In the 1890s suffragists' attempts to organize Southern states on behalf of woman suffrage met with some limited success. Until that time the bitterness of white Southerners over the prominent role of early women's rights leaders in the abolitionist movement made suffrage organization in the South nearly impossible. Now suffrage leaders faced a new decision. Should they cooperate with and hence tacitly condone Southern segregation practices in order to attract white Southerners to their cause? Suffragists almost never debated this question openly.[23] But a series of actions taken after 1890 reveals that white suffrage leaders chose to refrain from any challenge to Southern segregation practices in order to gain support from those white Southerners dedicated to the preservation of a white supremacist society.

Records of conventions of the National American Woman Suffrage Association (NAWSA) between 1894 and 1910 reflect this policy of cooperation with racism. In 1894 the NAWSA held its first convention in the South—in Atlanta, Georgia. Although Frederick Douglass had been an honored guest at association meetings for many years, Susan B. Anthony personally asked him not to attend the Atlanta convention. She feared that white Southerners newly interested in woman suffrage would be repulsed by any show of "social equality" between white women and blacks.[24]

At the 1899 national meeting a black delegate, Lottie Wilson Jackson, rose to propose the following resolution: "Be it resolved that colored women ought not to be compelled to ride in smoking cars, and that suitable accommodations should be provided for them."[25] Jackson explained that black women who sought to travel in the South were often forced to ride in a segregated section of filthy smoking cars, even when they had paid for better accommodations. Worse yet, some male smoking car passengers—uncouth, perhaps drunk—created an atmosphere in those cars that was repugnant to decent women. Railroad travel became so unpleasant for black women that many simply remained at home except in the most urgent situations.

---

[23]An exception was the correspondence that appeared in the *Woman's Journal* following the 1903 NAWSA meeting. The debate was touched off by a letter from William Lloyd Garrison, Jr., protesting the association's shameful silence about black rights. *Woman's Journal*, 2 May 1903, 140-41.

[24]Ida B. Wells, *Crusade for Justice: The Autobiography of Ida B. Wells*, ed. Alfreda M. Duster (Chicago: University of Chicago Press, 1970) 229-30.

[25]*Proceedings of the Thirty-first Annual Convention of the National American Woman Suffrage Association*, ed. Rachel Foster Avery (Warren OH: Press of Perry the Printer, 1899) 58.

White Southern delegates opposed the resolution vigorously. They charged that it was an inappropriate interference in the customs of one region of the country. They also claimed that suitable, but separate, accommodations on rail lines were generally provided for black women. After heated debate, NAWSA members voted to table the resolution on the grounds that it was beyond the legitimate scope of a woman suffrage group.

By voting to table the resolution, the majority of white delegates to that NAWSA convention showed that they were not willing to take even mild symbolic action to support the special priorities of black delegates. The issue of segregation in Jim Crow cars was an urgent issue for any black woman who needed to travel in the South. Confinement in separate cars meant considerable discomfort, especially on overnight trains that often had no berths available for black travelers. The *Woman's Era,* a black woman suffrage paper, described attempts to end the separate car system as "a matter of vital importance to every colored woman of the country." The editor warned, "There is no one among us, no matter what her culture or refinement, but who may become the victim of this iniquitous custom."[26] For more privileged black women the indignities of the separate car system were among the most painful manifestations of racism that they personally experienced.[27]

The separate car system *was* a woman's issue, because black women forced to travel in these separate cars were at risk of sexual harassment, sexual assault, and other forms of violence. Mary Church Terrell, traveling alone on a first-class ticket at the age of 16, was forced to move to the Jim Crow car. Other black passengers got off at early stops. As night approached, Terrell found herself alone in the car. She later recalled, "As young as I was, I had heard about awful tragedies which had overtaken colored girls who had been obliged to travel alone in these cars at night." Finally, after Terrell threatened that her wealthy father would sue the railroad company for failure to honor her first-class ticket, the conductor relented and allowed Terrell to join other passengers in the first-class car. Other black women did not escape in similar circumstances.[28]

The assaults on the spirits of black women traveling on the railroad system were as damaging as the threats to their bodies. Black educator and feminist Anna Julia Cooper vividly described the humiliation she suf-

---

[26]Untitled editorial, *Woman's Era,* February 1896, 10.

[27]Mary Church Terrell, *A Colored Woman in a White World* (Washington DC: Randall, 1940) 295. See also Charlotte Hawkins Brown, "Some Incidents in the Life and Career of Charlotte Hawkins Brown . . . ," Charlotte Hawkins Brown Papers, Schlesinger Library, Radcliffe College, Cambridge MA.

[28]Terrell, *A Colored Woman in a White World,* 297-99; Anna J. Cooper, *A Voice from the South* (Xenia OH: Aldine Printing House, 1892) 91.

fered as a black woman who frequently traveled in the South. "The feeling of slighted womanhood is unlike every other emotion of the soul. . . . Its poignancy . . . is holier than that of jealousy, deeper than indignation, tenderer than rage."[29] Apparently, white NAWSA delegates did not empathize enough with the feelings of slighted womanhood among their black colleagues to demand suitable accommodations for them on trains.

Denying the Charge of Promoting Social Equality

When the association's 1903 convention opened in New Orleans, suffragists were assailed by the local newspaper, the *Times-Democrat*. The paper alleged in an editorial that Southern women who worked for woman suffrage would be encouraging "social equality" between the races. The NAWSA board of officers, which included both Catt and Shaw, released a public reply, stating that the association had no official view on the question of equality for black Americans! Members' views on equality were entirely their private views, and members generally held those attitudes common in their own section of the country. National policy allowed state affiliates to organize their own groups in a manner consistent with the social practices of their state. That is to say, Southern chapters of the NAWSA could, and did, refuse to admit black members with the full knowledge of national officers. The statement continued,

> The National American Woman Suffrage Association is seeking to do away with the requirement of a sex qualification for suffrage. What other qualifications shall be asked for it leaves to each State. *The southern women most active in it have always in their own State emphasized the fact that granting suffrage to women who can read and write and who pay taxes would insure white supremacy* without resorting to any methods of doubtful constitutionality.[30]

The NAWSA board concluded by saying that it was unfair to single out the suffrage organization because its Northern and Western chapters admitted black members. Many other national organizations also admitted black members in other sections of the country. If the *Times-Democrat* wished to advise white women to avoid the NAWSA, it should also advise them to beware of Christianity, since Northern and Western churches were integrated.

At the same convention, the social equality issue was pressed upon Anna Howard Shaw in her popular nightly question-and-answer sessions. Finally, after ignoring written questions concerning this issue for several nights, she made the following response:

---

[29]Cooper, *Voice from the South*, 90-91.

[30]Ida H. Harper, ed., *The History of Woman Suffrage* (New York: National American Woman Suffrage Association, 1922) 5:59-60. Emphasis added.

You . . . disenfranchised both your black and your white women, thus making them politically equal. But you have put the ballot in the hands of your black men, thus making them the political superiors of your white women. Never before in the history of the world have men made former slaves the political masters of their former mistresses![31]

Instead of pandering to the prejudices of a white audience preoccupied by the specter of social equality, Shaw could have echoed the responses that black suffragists had developed to accusations that fairness to black citizens could be equated with "social equality." Those black suffragists stressed justice rather than ignoble comparisons between former slaves and their former mistresses. In her 1892 collection of essays Anna Julia Cooper distinguished clearly between the right of access to and civil treatment in public facilities, on the one hand, and, on the other, a coerced social intimacy. She insisted that "the social equality which means forced or unbidden association would be as much deprecated and as strenuously opposed by . . . [her black acquaintances] as by the most hide-bound Southerner."[32] Thus Southern women who were active in national associations that had black members would find that the black members declined to socialize with those white women whose disdain for them was readily apparent. Fannie Barrier Williams, a black lecturer and club leader, had told the 1893 World's Congress of Representative Women that "the social equality nonsense" did not originate in the black community. Indeed, the black community knew "that social equality can neither be enforced by law nor prevented by oppression." Blacks understood that "equality before the law, equality in the best sense of that term under our institutions, is totally different from social equality."[33]

Suppressing the Issue

In 1911 Martha Gruening, a white feminist who was an active supporter of black civil rights, tried to arrange for a black woman to introduce the following resolution at the upcoming NAWSA national convention:

Resolved, that women who are trying to lift themselves out of the class of the disfranchised, . . . express their sympathy with the black men and women who are fighting the same battle and recognize

[31]Anna Howard Shaw, *Story of a Pioneer* (New York: Harper and Brothers, 1915) 312.

[32]Cooper, *Voice from the South*, 111.

[33]Fannie Barrier Williams, "The Intellectual Progress of the Colored Women of the United States Since Emancipation," in *Black Women in Nineteenth-Century American Life*, ed. Bert James Loewenberg and Ruth Bogin (University Park PA: Pennsylvania State University Press, 1976) 277.

that it is as unjust and as undemocratic to disfranchise human beings on the ground of color as on the ground of sex.[34]

Anna Howard Shaw, president of the NAWSA, refused to accept Gruening's proposal. She opposed the presentation of the resolution because she felt that "we should [not] go into a Southern State to hold our national convention and then introduce any subject which we know beforehand will do nothing but create discord and inharmony in the convention." She warned, "The resolution which you proposed to introduce would do more to harm the success of our convention in Louisville than all of the other things that we do would do good." Shaw also stated that although she supported black people's right to vote, she resented what she perceived as heavy black male opposition to woman suffrage. "White women have no enemy in the world who does more to defeat our amendments, when submitted, than colored men."[35] Therefore, Shaw opposed what she viewed as a divisive resolution on behalf of the voting rights of men who contributed to the defeat of woman suffrage.

In 1916 suffrage leaders discussed plans to send representatives to the national conventions of the political parties in order to secure party support for the federal woman suffrage amendment. In private correspondence with Anna Howard Shaw, Carrie Chapman Catt commented, "Of course in the South the Republicans are mostly Negroes, and it will not do to induce them to go to Chicago. I suppose that would queer the whole suffrage movement in the South."[36]

In 1919 a group of black women's clubs called the Northeastern Federation of Women's Clubs applied to the NAWSA for admission as a co-operative member. Carrie Chapman Catt enlisted the help of white suffragist Ida Husted Harper to persuade the black federation to withdraw its application. Harper indicated that the votes of at least some Southern Democratic congressmen were essential to get the woman suffrage amendment passed. Supporters of woman suffrage believed that they had just exactly enough votes to get the amendment out of Congress. Harper warned, "if the news is flashed throughout the Southern States at this most critical moment that the National American Association has just admitted an organization of 6,000 colored women, the enemies can cease

---

[34]W. E. B. DuBois, "Suffering Suffragettes," *The Crisis,* June 1912, 77.

[35]Ibid. Shaw offered no evidence to support her claim that black men were especially strong in their opposition to woman suffrage. DuBois termed the accusation false.

[36]Catt to Shaw, 1 February 1916, Carrie Chapman Catt Papers, box 8, Library of Congress, Washington DC.

from further effort—the defeat of the Amendment will be assured."[37] The Northeastern Federation of Women's Clubs did agree to delay its application for one year, on the condition that the wording of the enforcement clause of the woman suffrage amendment pose no threat to black voting rights.

Black women were concerned about the enforcement clause of the woman suffrage amendment because in 1918 a change in that clause had been proposed as a parliamentary maneuver after the amendment in its usual form failed in Congress. The new wording left enforcement to the states, with the federal government reserving the power to intervene to promote enforcement if the states failed to take appropriate action. Some black civil rights activists were concerned about any measure that might diminish federal power to enforce voting rights. In 1918 the federal government was ignoring the disfranchisement of black men throughout the South. Any measure that further clouded the federal government's responsibility to protect black voting rights was particularly unwelcome.

In a letter to Carrie Chapman Catt, John R. Shillady of the NAACP warned that if the text of the woman suffrage amendment should "warrant us in believing that the Fifteenth Amendment would be weakened or imperilled, it would become our duty, in the interest of colored people . . . , to do all in our power to defeat the amendment."[38] This situation was the reverse of the situation created by the wording of the Fourteenth and Fifteenth Amendments. Now, supporters of black civil rights were threatening to work for the defeat of a woman suffrage amendment because its wording jeopardized black voting rights. Catt's response to Shillady was a terse statement that the enforcement language in its original form would be retained in the 1919 version; she made no explicit response to his threat nor did she express any opinion on black voting rights.[39]

While examples of racism are more evident, the woman suffrage movement was similarly involved in ethnic prejudice. Contempt for southern and eastern European and Asian immigrants who settled in America in large numbers after 1880 surfaced during the 1903 New Orleans meeting. Antagonism toward immigrants often was cloaked as support for stringent English language literacy tests as a prerequisite for the vote. The program for the 1903 NAWSA meeting included a panel discussion on educated suffrage. (At the turn of the century, persons met an educated suffrage requirement by demonstrating English language literacy; since political affairs were conducted in English, the ability to read

---

[37]Harper to Elizabeth C. Carter, 18 March 1919, NAACP Collection, group I, series C, box 407, Library of Congress, Washington DC.

[38]Shillady to Catt, 9 April 1919, ibid.

[39]Catt to Shillady, 11 April 1919, ibid.

Polish, Hebrew, or Chinese was not accepted as proof of literacy for suffrage purposes.) In the straw poll that ended the debate on educated suffrage, the audience voted overwhelmingly in favor of such a requirement. Only five women dissented. It should be noted that NAWSA officers did not take part since they were at a concurrent meeting. Also, Catt, who presided over the panel, put the question in terms of an educational qualification to be administered without regard to race. Nonetheless, the audience must have realized that far more immigrants and blacks than native-born American whites would be disfranchised should such a qualification be set.

In order to obtain increased social and political rights for women, Catt, Shaw, and their fellow suffrage leaders complied with segregationist practices in the Southern United States. They never challenged the validity of these practices openly. Indeed, they attempted to avoid any discussion of the race question insofar as that was possible.

Manipulating Racial and Ethnic Stereotypes

On some occasions suffrage leaders did more than passively cooperate with segregationists. Sometimes they utilized arguments for woman suffrage that were explicitly racist and nativist. They appealed in racial terms to the Anglo-Saxon males who controlled access to the ballot box.

Stanton feared the enfranchisement of black men (without accompanying full female suffrage) because she viewed "degraded" black men as even more prone to oppress women than were Saxon men. When she came into conflict with black men, her own feelings of superiority came to the fore. Particularly noticeable was her tendency to refer to blacks by the demeaning nicknames Sambo and Dinah. In 1869 Frederick Douglass chided Stanton for exhibiting racial and class bias in an address.

> There was in the address to which I allude, a sentiment in reference to employment and certain names, such as "Sambo" and the gardener and the boot black and the daughters of Jefferson and Washington. . . . I have asked what difference there is between the daughters of Jefferson and Washington and other daughters.[40]

Stanton's racial prejudice was also evident in her response to white women who were trying to gain woman suffrage through state by state appeals to male voters, including blacks and immigrants. She predicted that white women forced to listen to the "puerile objections" of black men and immigrants and to "parley with them [blacks and immigrants] on their own low ground" would soon be "stung into . . . dignified self respect."[41] She

[40]"Annual Meeting of the American Equal Rights Association," *The Revolution*, 21 May 1869, 306.

[41]"Anniversary of the National Woman Suffrage Association," *The Revolution*, 18 May 1870, 305.

anticipated that these Anglo-Saxon women, humiliated by encounters with their inferiors, would soon see the wisdom of seeking a federal amendment enfranchising women, for a federal amendment could be secured through contact with one's own kind of man—an educated, Anglo-Saxon congressman or state legislator.

Later in her life Stanton became an ardent advocate of educated suffrage. One of the sources of her conversion to this position was her fear of the immigrants newly arrived from southern and eastern Europe whom she repeatedly characterized in stereotypical terms. Frightened because she believed the new immigrants to be "the dregs of Europe," she advocated a five-year residency requirement coupled with an English language literacy test. During the five-year probationary period, immigrants were to learn both the dominant language and the political customs of America. Such a regulation would enhance the stability of the state, for "a law compelling all our foreign citizens to read and write the English language would make our whole people more homogeneous and united."[42] Though Stanton was fearful of immigrants who were ignorant of the American system, she also intended for the literacy requirement that she proposed to be justly administered. It was "an educational qualification for all voters, black and white, foreign and native, men and women."[43]

Stanton outlined her position on educated suffrage in detail in an 1895 article entitled "Our Proper Attitude Toward Immigration." While she welcomed immigrants who were "honest, industrious, intelligent, moral," she feared that many of the more recent immigrants were a great deal less than that. Indeed, she proclaimed, "There are immigration societies in England for the express purpose of shipping her criminals, paupers, idiots, maimed, halt and blind, deaf and dumb here."[44] She criticized the British for neglecting their responsibility to care for their weak and to restrain their evil citizens—for shifting to American social institutions almost unbearable burdens. Stanton charged that these unpromising newcomers lacked the basic skills necessary for integration into American life. She alleged they could not read or write, did not grasp the basic principles of democratic government, and lacked an appreciation of true liberty as opposed to license. Lacking comprehension of that distinction, some among the new immigrants fomented discontent as socialists or anarchists. Stanton declared that such socialists would be better employed

---

[42]"Letter," *Woman's Journal,* 3 November 1894, 348.

[43]"Educated Suffrage Symposium," *Woman's Journal,* 2 October 1897, 313.

[44]Elizabeth Cady Stanton, "Our Proper Attitude Toward Immigration," *American Woman's Journal,* March-April 1895, 91 (clipping in Elizabeth Cady Stanton Papers, box 7, Library of Congress, Washington DC).

changing conditions in the European countries from which they came, not disrupting American life.

Worst of all, in Stanton's opinion, foreign-born men voted against woman suffrage. In self-defense, native-born American women should oppose any further extension of the suffrage to foreign men until they themselves secured the franchise. As Stanton summarized her position: women demand a halt to any further extension of the suffrage to foreign-born or native-born men, especially to the uneducated, until upper classes of women are enfranchised. "There can be no question as to the comparative benefit to the State of the votes of intelligent, native-born women or the votes of ignorant, foreign-born men."[45]

Suffragists not only compromised with racism and ethnic prejudices in organizing on behalf of the vote; they also turned such prejudices into a tool with which to earn the franchise. They argued explicitly that woman suffrage would benefit society since it would ensure Anglo-Saxon dominance at the polls. Clearly, suffragists had moved a long way from their original stress on women's full participation in a society justly based on the consent of *all* the governed.

---

[45]Ibid., 91-92.

2 | Racism and Nativism

WHITE SUFFRAGISTS chose to manipulate the Anglo-Saxon mystique in order to promote woman suffrage. In the late nineteenth century there was a prevalent belief (among whites of Germanic ancestry) that Anglo-Saxons were uniquely qualified to create good governments. In such a milieu, suffragists who wanted to argue their case had only to show that the net result of woman suffrage would be to increase the proportion of Anglo-Saxon voters in the electorate.

Nineteenth-Century Racism

How had Americans of Anglo-Saxon ancestry come, by the end of the nineteenth century, to convince themselves that their ethnic group was superior to all others? Racism has a long history in America. The original colonists believed themselves superior to the uncivilized heathen, the Native Americans they found in the new land, and also to the blacks they imported as slaves. Their sense of superiority was strengthened by the Puritan belief that God had commissioned them to establish a model society in this new land. Controversy soon arose over the extent to which blacks and Indians could participate in that society.

During the era that preceded the Civil War, apologists for Southern society harped upon the racial inferiority of blacks. They described slavery as a system necessary to integrate the intrinsically inferior black race into Southern life. Even some abolitionists made clear that they regarded the blacks as inferior beings. While blacks should be free, they could not and should not become equal members of the society.

By the last quarter of the nineteenth century this Anglo-Saxon supremacist ideology was reaching its crest in American thought.

> The fact is that the atmosphere of the late nineteenth century was so thoroughly permeated with racist thought (reinforced by Darwinism) that few men managed to escape it. The idea that certain cultures and races were naturally inferior . . . was almost universally held by educated, middle-class, respectable Americans.[1]

Widespread belief in Anglo-Saxon superiority appeared to be supported

---

[1]Christopher Lasch, "The Anti-Imperialists, the Phillipines and the Inequality of Man," *Journal of Southern History* 24 (1958): 330.

firmly by impressive scholarship. A wide variety of academic disciplines seemed to be uncovering evidence of Anglo-Saxon supremacy. By the late nineteenth century, notions of innate racial superiority were an important feature of academic fields such as biology, political science, history, and linguistics.

Philologists, investigating the origin of the modern languages, had discovered similarities among Sanskrit, Greek, Latin, German, English, and Celtic. This led scholars to posit the existence of a primitive people labeled Aryans, who spoke an original language from which the others were derived. Scholars further hypothesized that these Aryans spread their language as they moved westward across Europe and that they made distinctive contributions to Western civilizations as they advanced. Observed similarities among languages were parlayed into a portrait of a blond super-race which spread its virtues as well as its language throughout the Western world.

Historians joined philologists in probing the history of early Germanic tribes. Many seized upon the flattering portrait that the Roman historian Tacitus had drawn of those peoples. A repetition and elaboration of Germanic virtues became a nineteenth-century historical staple. The Germanic people were described as courageous, independent, freedom-loving, and unusually gifted in politics and law. The Anglo-Saxon school of history presented these traits as hereditary racial characteristics. These historians marshaled evidence to show that descendants of the Germanic peoples had continued to demonstrate a unique talent for self-government.

American historians put special emphasis on tracing American political practices back to Teutonic, Norman, or Anglo-Saxon origins. Some compared democratic institutions, such as the New England town meeting, to Germanic tribal customs. Other historians studied Anglo-Saxon law as the precursor of modern constitutional law. But historians went beyond an attempt to show that American institutions had roots that reached back to early Germanic times when they "assumed that the ability to create these institutions was imbedded in the biological character of the Teutonic or Anglo-Saxon race."[2]

In the late nineteenth century political science was still closely related to history. Representative of the period's racist scholarship is the then influential text *Political Science and Comparative Constitutional Law*. Its author, John W. Burgess, asserted that nationality groups, like individuals, display unique talents. Teutonic people had demonstrated a unique capacity for stable government. Even in European countries where they were a minority of the population, it was the Teutonic citizens who had con-

---

[2]Thomas Gossett, *Race: The History of an Idea in America* (Dallas: Southern Methodist University Press, 1963) 138.

structed effective political institutions. This unique talent for government created an obligation on the part of Teutonic peoples. They were obliged to intervene to form good governments in nations peopled by politically inferior races. Within a nation, political stability was increased when the population was homogeneous. If inferior stock was present, the political power of that group should be held to a minimum. Burgess made clear the implications of this notion.

> The Teutonic nations can never regard the exercise of political power as the right of man. With them this capacity must be based upon capacity to discharge political duty, and they themselves are the best organs which have as yet appeared to determine when and where this capacity exists.[3]

The publication of Darwin's *Origin of Species* in 1859 was a key event in the history of racist thought. Darwin offered a coherent theory of evolution that allowed scientists to explain differences among human beings as well as among animals. While Darwin himself was not interested in using his concepts systematically to explore observed or assumed human racial differences, others were.[4] Thus, the last half of the nineteenth century saw the rise of Social Darwinism, the theory of the evolution of human groups loosely based upon Darwin's work.

> The most popular catchwords of Darwinism, "struggle for existence" and "survival of the fittest," when applied to the life of man in society, suggested that nature would provide that the best competitors in a competitive situation would win, and that this process would lead to continuing improvement.[5]

Social Darwinists believed that human society is evolving in a process controlled by immutable laws of nature. This process of evolution leads human groups to ever higher states of civilization. The evolutionary process appears to be fueled by natural selection. In situations of social and economic competition human beings or groups with naturally superior

---

[3]John W. Burgess, *Political Science and Comparative Constitutional Law* (Boston: Ginn & Company, 1890) 1:45.

[4]Herbert Spencer was the social philosopher who, much more than Darwin, was interested in the contribution of evolutionary theory to an understanding of human society. Spencer's work was widely known in America. Citations in Stanton's writings show that she had read Spencer. Spencer's influence on Catt's personal philosophy can be gauged by the fact that at the time of her death, in 1947, she still considered a copy of his collected works an important part of her personal library.

[5]Richard Hofstadter, *Social Darwinism in American Thought* (Boston: Beacon Press, 1955) 6.

attributes inevitably rise to positions of dominance while persons or groups with naturally inferior characteristics remain subordinate or even die out.

Social Darwinism is a harsh, but not necessarily racist, social philosophy. However, the late nineteenth century was also heir to a body of scientific research on human racial and ethnic differences. Since 1735, when Carl Linnaeus had published his *Systema Naturae,* biologists had been busy classifying living beings according to precise categories, notably species and genera. Some scientists specialized in classifying human beings into categories based on ethnic characteristics and physical measurements. Descriptions of the various human types contained observations about personality characteristics as well as physical attributes.

> The books described, and even pictured, the racial traits of Laplanders and Berbers, Magyars and Japanese, Teutons and Hottentots, Anglo-Saxons and Slavs. In tables of impressive statistics, carried to two or more decimal places, could be found exact measurements of these peoples' social, physical and cultural qualities.[6]

Racial prejudice heavily biased some of these typologies. When theories of racial difference were mixed in the popular mind with Social Darwinism, the Anglo-Saxons came to be viewed as the superiors in the struggle for survival, and other races and nationalities became inferiors. Science "proved" not only Indians, Negroes, and Orientals, but also Slavs, Jews, Italians, and Poles to be inferior peoples.

During the last quarter of the nineteenth century the white racism that gripped both popular thought and scholarship surfaced during debates on public policy. Political figures who advocated a retreat from Reconstruction era protection of black civil rights appealed to common stereotypes of the ignorant, irresponsible, sexually immoral, dishonest, even bestial Negro. Rayford Logan's work shows that this was a picture with which the politician could assume his listeners—Northerners or Southerners—were familiar, for the popular press of the day widely disseminated a demeaning image of blacks.[7] Belief in the natural inferiority of the Negro race was so widespread that few voices were raised to challenge Supreme Court decisions detrimental to blacks, black male disfranchisement throughout the South, passage of Jim Crow codes, or reconciliation between North and South purchased at the expense of blacks.

Racism figured equally prominently in debates over American imperialism. "In the decades after 1885, Anglo-Saxonism, belligerent or pa-

---

[6]Oscar Handlin, *Race and Nationality in American Life* (Garden City NJ: Doubleday & Co., Anchor Books, 1957) 71.

[7]See Rayford W. Logan, *The Negro in American Life and Thought: The Nadir, 1877-1901* (New York: Dial Press, 1954).

cific, was the dominant abstract rationale of American imperialism."[8] As a result of the Spanish-American War and other international ventures, America faced a troublesome question. What role should the United States play in the governance of territories peopled primarily by non-Caucasians? Some political figures roused Americans with cries of the "white man's burden." On the theory that Anglo-Saxons had demonstrated a unique capacity for good government, these men spoke of America's moral duty to provide stable political institutions for inferior races newly brought under American influence. American "Anglo-Saxons" should rule benevolently over their colored brothers and sisters, providing them with the social institutions that might mitigate their barbarism.

While some opponents challenged these racist assertions, other anti-imperialists objected to American foreign policy on equally racist grounds.[9] They pointed out that American political principles mandated that all citizens have a voice in government. Thus, if Hawaiians, Cubans, Filipinos, and others came under direct United States control, they, too, would be entitled to the vote. But, as members of inferior racial groups, these new people were incapable of responsible participation in government. Thus, direct governmental supervision of these territories presented a dilemma: either compromise treasured political principles or pollute the voter pool with inferior stock. Anti-imperialists suggested that the United States withdraw from these areas and leave the inferior people there to fend for themselves.

White woman suffragists, who shared many of the racial and ethnic prejudices of their peers, appealed to the Anglo-Saxon mystique to further their own cause. They asserted that woman suffrage would guarantee continued Anglo-Saxon domination of government, a dominance that was being challenged during the final half of the nineteenth century by the enfranchisement of former slave men and by immigration from southern and eastern European countries. Suffragists presented census figures showing large numbers of women of Anglo-Saxon descent available to strengthen that group's power at the polls.

Bolstering Anglo-Saxon Political Dominance

White Supremacy

In 1919 Carrie Chapman Catt suggested that woman suffrage would be an acceptable means to maintain Anglo-Saxon political dominance.

---

[8]Hofstadter, *Social Darwinism*, 172.

[9]Anna Howard Shaw in a speech entitled "The White Man's Burden" challenged such racist assumptions (Shaw Papers, box 22, folder 502, Dillon Collection, Schlesinger Library, Radcliffe College, Cambridge MA). Others who challenged this racism are mentioned in Hofstadter, *Social Darwinism*, 166-68, and Gossett, *Race*, 334-36.

Using 1910 census data, she demonstrated that the proportion of women to be enfranchised was higher among native-born groups than among immigrant groups. Since immigrant groups tended to be more heavily male, they had less to gain from woman suffrage. Female enfranchisement would minimize the power of foreign-born voters.

Catt also met forthrightly Southern fears that enfranchised black women would pose a threat to white supremacy. "White supremacy," she replied, "will be strengthened, not weakened, by woman suffrage."[10] She cited population figures for the entire South which showed that the number of white women exceeded the number of black women by over 4 million—a ratio of two to one. In fact, the white female population of the South exceeded the entire black population, both male and female. Potentially, white women voters could offset the entire black vote across the South.

Catt's *Objections to the Federal Amendment* contained a table of white and black population figures for each Southern state. Only in South Carolina and Mississippi did black women outnumber white women, and in both of those states the number of black men already exceeded the number of white men, so woman suffrage posed no additional threat to the balance of power between the races. Catt reassured residents of Mississippi and South Carolina that literacy and poll tax qualifications for voters currently in force in their states would apply to women should they be enfranchised. Thus, the same tactics being used to disfranchise black males would be effective against black females. Again, woman suffrage would not be a threat to white supremacy in any state.

Finally, Catt drew attention to the dubious constitutionality of grandfather clauses being used in some Southern states to maintain white political power. She quoted a North Carolina jurist to the effect that enfranchised white women could stand as a bulwark of white dominance if the United States Supreme Court should strike down such clauses. Catt suggested that Southern states would find woman suffrage a valuable weapon in its white supremacy arsenal.

Catt carefully documented her claims that the vote for women would enhance Anglo-Saxon political power. Stanton, too, had urged woman suffrage as a means to maintain Anglo-Saxon dominance. When she ran for Congress, Stanton warned her constituents, "In view of the fact that Freedmen of the South and the millions of foreigners now crowding our shores . . . are all in the progress of events to be enfranchised, the best interests of the nation demand that we outweigh this incoming pauperism, ignorance, and degradation, with the wealth, education, and refinement

---

[10]Carrie Chapman Catt, *Objections to the Federal Amendment* (New York: National Woman Suffrage Publishing Co., 1919) 10.

of the women of the republic."[11] Stanton did not offer any specific figures to support her claim that, as a result of the enfranchisement of women, the native-born vote would continue to outweigh the foreign-born vote; she merely assumed that it would and that native-born dominance would be desirable.

Daughters of Jefferson

Catt and Stanton insisted that woman suffrage would benefit society since it would increase the proportion of Anglo-Saxon voters at the polls. Anglo-Saxon voters were alleged to be superior participants in government because they understood better the mechanism of democratic government and because they were less easily manipulated by corrupt politicians.

White, native-born suffragists pointed out that freedmen and immigrants had lived under slavery, monarchy, or despotism. Neither experience nor education had prepared them to enter effectively into the democratic process. Some suffragists were particularly concerned that such men did not understand the principles, history, and traditions of America's political system. Catt complained before Congress that suffragists were "compelled to petition men who have never heard of the Declaration of Independence, and who have never read the constitution."[12] Shaw admitted to the House Judiciary Committee that she lacked faith in "the men who come from the Old World, who know nothing of our public institutions, who do not comprehend the principles underlying our Government, and who have not been reared in our spirit of freedom."[13] Stanton expressed a similar concern about the political impact of the foreign vote. She feared that laws were being made by men who did not understand even the most basic aspects of the American system.

White, native-born suffragists portrayed immigrants and freedmen as ill-equipped to contribute to the nation's welfare. In sharp contrast, they argued that Anglo-Saxon women were unusually well trained for self-

---

[11]Elizabeth Cady Stanton, Susan B. Anthony, and Mathilda J. Gage, eds., *The History of Woman Suffrage* (New York: Fowler and Wells, 1882) 2:181. This quote is an example of a favorite rhetorical device of suffragists. Foreign-born male voters described in the worst possible light (as poor, ignorant, vicious) are contrasted with native-born women seen in the best possible light (as virtuous, well-educated, and wealthy). Those native-born citizens who were ill-equipped to vote went unmentioned as did the foreign-born women who stood to gain the vote.

[12]"Hearing Before Senate 1900," Carrie Chapman Catt Papers, box 10, Library of Congress, Washington DC.

[13]Wilmer A. Linkugel, "The Speeches of Anna Howard Shaw: Collected and Edited with Introduction and Notes," 2 vols. (Ph.D. diss., University of Wisconsin, 1961) 2:698.

government. Stanton described potential women voters as direct descendants of those men who had designed American political institutions. They were the heirs of the Pilgrims and the signers of the Declaration of Independence. By implication, native-born women had an intimate knowledge of American government and would make particularly astute voters. Catt described the women who pressed for a share in government as "daughters of Revolutionary fathers" who "in their childhood homes had learned the meaning of political freedom."[14]

Stanton also pointed to the cultural experience of native-born women as creating a special fitness for the vote. Like native-born men, such women were "born of the same parents, reared under the same flag, reading the same national history and arguments for Justice, Liberty and Equality; singing the same songs of freedom; worshiping the same God who created man and woman in his own image, simultaneously, and gave them equal dominion over every living thing, an equal title deed to this green earth."[15]

As native-born women, many black feminists could also claim a similarly distinguished American heritage. For example, Fannie Barrier Williams described black women as the daughters of men who had been intensely loyal to the fundamental principles of the American Republic. In particular, she asked, "Do these women not belong to a race that has never faltered in its support of the country's flag in every war since Attucks fell in Boston's streets?"[16] Black women, too, were the daughters of revolutionary war fathers.

A Purchasable Vote?

According to many white woman suffrage leaders, white, American-born women had the background which befits a good voter. They charged, however, that immigrant men and freedmen were poorly equipped to vote. Therefore, the welfare of the state would be advanced if woman suffrage were used as a means to ensure that native-born whites could outvote the undesirables. Concretely, many white suffragists asserted that the votes of native-born white women were needed in the fight against political corruption. White, native-born women could offset the votes of immigrant and black men, who seemed readily manipulated by dishonest politicians.

---

[14]Carrie Chapman Catt and Nettie R. Shuler, *Woman Suffrage and Politics* (1926; reprint ed., Seattle: University of Washington Press, 1969) 162.

[15]Elizabeth Cady Stanton, "Women Do Not Wish to Vote," *National Bulletin* 2 (April 1894): 3.

[16]Fannie Barrier Williams, "The Intellectual Progress of the Colored Women of the United States Since Emancipation," in *Black Women in Nineteenth-Century American Life,* ed. Bert James Loewenberg and Ruth Bogin (University Park PA: Pennsylvania State University Press, 1976) 276.

Catt described immigrant men as a group especially vulnerable to un-scrupulous politicians. As early as 1890 she alleged a connection between growing immigration and the increasing power of political bosses, most of whom, she claimed, were either immigrants themselves or children of immigrants. According to Catt, immigrants—often unable to understand campaign issues discussed in an alien tongue—would sell their votes for a job, a political favor, or even liquor or money. She made it clear that it was not the immigrant's strangeness, but his vulnerability to corruption that was the problem. "The danger lies not so much in the fact that it is an alien vote as that it is an ignorant and controlled vote."[17]

Catt believed that black men were also unusually prone to political corruption. She told one suffrage convention that disfranchisement of blacks throughout the South was being tolerated because the Negro vote appeared to be a "purchasable vote." Now, Northern politicians were be-ginning to follow the lead of Southerners—buying the vote in black pre-cincts.[18]

Fear of the immigrant and Negro vote drove both Catt and Stanton to contradict their own assertions that all persons knew their own interests best and thus should be allowed to vote. Both claimed that freedmen and men fresh from steerage were so confused by their new lives that they could not perceive their own good clearly. Stanton's judgment concerning the political wisdom of immigrants was negative: faced with complex legisla-tive proposals, she charged, immigrants had shown themselves incapable of judging where their own best interests lay. "The logical sequence of un-wise legislation is not so easily traced by the undisciplined mind that he can readily see what measures would promote his own interests."[19]

Stanton also described black men as the pawns first of the Republican party and then of the Democratic party. She believed that Southern ex-perience had proven black men incapable of advancing their own inter-ests through independent voting practices. These statements represent a departure from Stanton's earlier position; during the early Reconstruc-tion period she had asserted that if certain classes were not using their votes effectively on their own behalf, the solution was education in civic pro-cedures, not benevolent rule by upper classes.

---

[17]"The American Sovereign," Carrie Chapman Catt Papers, box 3, Astor, Lenox, and Tilden Foundations, Rare Books and Manuscript Division, New York Public Library.

[18]Carrie Chapman Catt, *President's Annual Address Delivered Before the Thirty-fourth Annual Convention of the National American Woman Suffrage Association* (Washing-ton: Hayworth Publishing House, n.d.) 9.

[19]Elizabeth Cady Stanton, "An Open Letter," *Woman's Journal,* 5 February 1898, 42.

Black suffragists responded sharply to accusations that the black vote was a purchasable vote. They drew attention to the social conditions under which black men in the South sometimes took money in return for agreeing to vote for a particular candidate: many Southern black men were desperately poor; black men who cast an independent ballot were often threatened with or suffered physical violence; corruption was widespread; honest black votes were frequently uncounted. In 1891 black suffragist Frances Ellen Watkins Harper warned the National Council of Women of the United States that the government could not allow the political corruption and violence in the South to continue without undermining democracy itself. "Men cannot vitiate his [the black man's] vote by fraud, or intimidate the voter by violence, without being untrue to the genius and spirit of our government." Mary Church Terrell had just such corrupt conditions in mind when she told the 1904 NAWSA convention that black men "never sold their vote till they found that it made no difference how they cast them." In her 1891 speech Harper reminded her hearers that black men were ignorant because they were the victims of a slavery system that made it a crime to teach a slave how to read. Since the Civil War, black men and women in great numbers had learned to read. Should black people be denied the vote because they were poor and did not share the stable social perspective of the property owner? Harper responded, "If he is poor, what has become of the money he has been earning for the last two hundred and fifty years?" It was, she claimed, the labor of black people on the plantations of the South and in the factories of the North that was the foundation of national prosperity. Since black persons had been unjustly deprived of the material and educational resources that are the foundation of good political judgment, the solution, according to Harper, was to redress these wrongs, rather than to compound them by depriving black men of the vote. "Instead of taking the ballot from his hands, teach him how to use it, and to add his quota to the progress, strength, and durability of the nation."[20] The portion of Harper's 1891 speech that discusses Negro suffrage is very similar to Elizabeth Cady Stanton's 1867 plea for universal suffrage before the New York state legislature. It was a tragedy that by 1891 Stanton had lost faith in the argument that Harper now put forward.

White suffragists bolstered their claim to the ballot by arguing that while black and immigrant men fell prey to the bosses, white native-born women could not be controlled through any of the normal tactics favored by machine politicians. Stanton insisted that political bosses opposed

---

[20]Frances Ellen Watkins Harper, "Duty to Dependent Races," in *Black Women in Nineteenth-Century American Life*, ed. Loewenberg and Bogin, 248-50; Paula Giddings, *When and Where I Enter: The Impact of Black Women on Race and Sex in America* (New York: William Morrow and Company, 1984) 122.

woman suffrage because women were among those "whose votes they could not manipulate to maintain the present conditions of injustice and oppression in every department of life." Catt and Shaw concurred in the opinion that corrupt political leaders feared woman suffrage. Shaw believed that industrial trusts and politicians under the control of the liquor interests especially feared the reform measures women voters would demand. "There is nothing the foes of decency and good order dread more than the votes of women and a jury of mothers."[21]

Some black suffragists agreed that black women as women were less vulnerable to the blandishments of corrupt politicians. W. E. B. DuBois believed that black women's somewhat greater job opportunities and hence somewhat greater economic security made them less vulnerable to political bribes. "You can bribe some pauperized Negro laborers with a few dollars at election time, but you cannot bribe a Negro woman." Anna Julia Cooper claimed that the black woman had astute judgment about the political policies which benefited the black race; "you do not find the colored woman selling her birthright for a mess of pottage."[22]

"Patrick and Sambo and Hans and Yung Tung"

The argument that Anglo-Saxon women, if enfranchised, would bring to the polls a thorough knowledge of governmental principles and an immunity to political corruption degenerated at times into the inference that Anglo-Saxon women would make good voters simply because they were Anglo-Saxon. Native-born white women were sometimes pictured as superior beings by virtue of their race. Conversely, black men, Native American men, and men from southern and eastern Europe were portrayed as innately inferior citizens.

As early as 1869 Stanton appealed to racial and ethnic prejudice when she urged, "American women of wealth, virtue and refinement, if you do not wish the lower orders of Chinese, Africans, Germans and Irish, with their low ideas of womanhood to make laws for you . . . demand that woman, too, shall be represented in the government." A few weeks later she reminded her readers that American women found it difficult enough "to bear the oppressions of their own Saxon Fathers, the best orders of manhood." Unless they obtained the suffrage, she warned, they were faced with the far more repulsive prospect of rule by "Patrick and Sambo and Hans and Yung Tung."[23]

---

[21]"The Degradation of Disfranchisement," Elizabeth Cady Stanton Papers, box 10, Library of Congress, Washington DC; Linkugel, "Speeches of Shaw," 2:750.

[22]Giddings, *When and Where I Enter*, 123; Anna J. Cooper, *A Voice from the South* (Xenia OH: Aldine Printing House, 1892) 139.

[23]"The Sixteenth Amendment," *The Revolution*, 29 April 1869, 266; "Anniversary of the American Equal Rights Association," *The Revolution*, 13 May 1869, 291.

In 1884 Stanton described an incident in which women were turned away from the polls: "Intelligent American women were crowded aside, by burly African men, who could neither read nor write."[24] This statement was carefully contrived to play on the prejudices of her audience. Actually, a group of women voters had presented themselves to registrars in the District of Columbia, asserting that under the Fourteenth Amendment women as citizens had a right to vote. The election officials were unwilling to accept that interpretation of the amendment and refused to permit the women to cast their ballots. They did, however, allow black men who were indisputably enfranchised to vote. Black men had not pushed white women aside either figuratively or literally.

White suffragists made comparisons with black men that were demeaning to those black men. They also *failed to make comparisons* that would have drawn attention to the oppression of black men. When white suffragists spoke of the disfranchised they rarely mentioned black men, who were being stripped of their right to vote during the closing years of the nineteenth century. They rarely commented upon the systematic degradation of black Americans or the rising tide of violence against blacks. Yet the closing quarter of the nineteenth century was the period when black men were disfranchised, Jim Crow codes were fully elaborated, federal protection of black rights was totally withdrawn, the Supreme Court affirmed the legitimacy of separate but equal, and lynching increased tremendously. The last decade of the nineteenth century, "more than . . . any other time since the Civil War, . . . was an era demanding consistent and principled protest against racism."[25] Yet, given the horrors of the times, Shaw, Stanton, and Catt were distressingly silent about racial injustice.[26] They continued to emphasize woman suffrage as *the* suffrage issue, ignoring the disfranchisement of black men.

White suffragists attempted to move Anglo-Saxon men to support suffrage for Anglo-Saxon women by drawing lurid contrasts between the political situation of white women and Native American men as well as white women and black men. In an early speech, "Subject and Sovereign," Catt drew a sharp contrast between the political status of white women settlers and men from the Sioux tribes in South Dakota. While she manifested occasional glimmers of sympathy for the Indians, her overriding tone was hostile. Catt found it unacceptable that Native American men, at best a few steps away from barbarism, were offered powers of citizen-

---

[24]Clipping, Susan B. Anthony Collection, Rare Book Collection, Library of Congress, Washington DC.

[25]Angela Davis, *Women, Race and Class* (New York: Random House, 1981) 112.

[26]My attention was initially drawn to this point in a conversation with Peter Paris of Vanderbilt University.

ship denied to college-educated, Anglo-Saxon women. Catt, aware of the ghost dance—symbol of a religious revival sweeping through the Sioux in the 1890s—used an allusion to that event as a demonstration that Indians were incapable of rational judgment. Her fear and contempt of Indians were summarized in her lament that the United States had "opened the gate to every murdering, scalping warrior among them to all the privileges and immunities of American citizenship."[27] The clear inference of Catt's speech was that the patriotic, self-sufficient white women of South Dakota would make far better voters than did Native American men.

Descriptions by Shaw and Catt of Indians they observed while campaigning in South Dakota in 1890 perpetuated the notion that such men were less capable of self-government than were white women. The two leaders dwelt on facets of the Indians' appearance that seemed to mark them as uncivilized. Catt recoiled from the respect shown to the three Sioux delegates to the Republican convention. They appeared, she said, "with the moccasins still on their feet and their long dishevelled hair so full of inhabitants you could see them clear across the room." Shaw, too, was repulsed by "Indians whose degree of civilization was indicated by their warpaint and the flaunting feathers of their headdresses."[28]

While Shaw was repelled by the fact that Native American men whom she considered uncivilized were granted a share in government while superbly qualified white women were disfranchised, she recognized that Anglo-Saxons could claim no innate moral superiority over Indians. In a late nineteenth-century speech, she pointed out that the generosity of many Native Americans toward the earliest American colonists had been met with brutality. Reflecting on the then recent conflict at Wounded Knee, South Dakota, she excoriated the Army for its slaughter of Indian women and children. Again, while speaking in Seattle, she honored Sacajawea, the Indian woman who had guided the Lewis and Clark Expedition to the Pacific. Picturing the evils done to Native Americans by the white race, Shaw entreated, "May we, the daughters of an alien race who slew your people and usurped your country, learn the lessons of calm endurance, of patient persistence and unfaltering courage exemplified in

---

[27]"Subject and Sovereign," Carrie Chapman Catt Papers, box 3, New York Public Library. Some Indians caught up in the ghost dance did engage in very excited forms of behavior—trances, visions, and so forth. See James Mooney, *The Ghost Dance Religion and the Sioux Outbreak of 1890* (Chicago: University of Chicago Press, 1965) 185-99. However, Sioux behavior was no more irrational than behavior displayed by those attending fervent revival meetings. If the Sioux were unfit to vote, so were many white Americans.

[28]"Subject and Sovereign," Carrie Chapman Catt Papers, box 3, New York Public Library; Anna Howard Shaw, *The Story of a Pioneer* (New York: Harper and Brothers, 1915) 252.

your life, in our efforts to lead men through the Pass of justice."[29] Such passages reveal that Shaw had no narrow notion of the racial superiority of any group.

According to some white, native-born feminists, not only was it unfitting that uncivilized Native American men should vote while white American women did not, it was also unjust that the franchise should be extended to foreign-born men while it was withheld from native-born women. Throughout the 1890s Catt decried the wave of new immigration drawn increasingly from southern and eastern Europe. She expressed concern that immigrants in this period were coming from areas plagued with illiteracy, poverty, and crime. She made the stereotypical accusation that America was becoming a dumping ground for all the world's evil elements. Catt invited her audience to inspect the people coming through Ellis Island—to note "those faces hardened with crime and stolid with ignorance."[30]

Stanton's testimony before a Senate Committee on Woman Suffrage contained a similar description of immigrants' features. The steerage passengers on an Atlantic crossing she had recently made were "dull-eyed, heavy-visaged, stooping with huge burdens and the oppressions they endured in the Old World." The realization that these men were soon to become her political masters saddened and frightened Stanton. Her testimony continued with a plea to those Saxon men who were her equals to save *their* women from rule by inferiors. When other suffragists proposed a resolution praising legislators who supported bills favorable to women, Stanton retorted that she refused gratitude to men who allowed the Anglo-Saxon woman's right to self-government to be "trodden into the dust by the wooden shoed peasantry of Russia, Germany, Norway, and Sweden."[31] Stanton was disgusted that Anglo-Saxon women were being governed in part by inferior foreigners—men who were ignorant, poor, and vicious.

Professional Status and Refinement

The argument that woman suffrage would rightfully secure power in the hands of society's better element was rooted in class bias as well as racial and ethnic prejudice. Suffragists most often revealed class bias through references to occupation. They asserted that it was unfair for upper-class

---

[29]Anna Howard Shaw, "Indians versus Women," *Woman's Tribune*, 9 May 1891, 146-47; Linkugel, "Speeches of Shaw," 2:437.

[30]"The American Sovereign," Carrie Chapman Catt Papers, box 3, New York Public Library.

[31]U.S. Congress, Senate, Committee on Woman Suffrage, *Hearings before the Committee on Woman Suffrage*, 50th Cong., 2d sess., 1888, p. 8; "Letter to Worchester Convention," *Woman's Tribune*, 31 January 1891, 34.

women to be governed by unskilled workers or servants. In an 1867 speech Stanton declared that Southern white women occupied a more dignified position than did their Northern counterparts. In the South black workers from the lowest strata were still disfranchised and hence not the rulers of upper-class women, while in the North men from all groups governed women. "In the Southern States the women were not . . . humiliated in seeing their coachmen, gardeners, and waiters go to the polls to legislate on their interests."[32] Nearly a quarter of a century later, Stanton was still requesting sarcastically that women be elevated to political equality with their gardeners and coachmen. Catt made the same appeal by contrasting disfranchised professional women with enfranchised unskilled workers. "Do you realize," she asked, "that such anomalies as a College President asking her janitor to give her a vote are . . . driving women to desperation?"[33] Catt's comment conveyed the impression that men from certain groups, such as janitors, were unsuited to pass judgment on the political destiny of their betters.

At times Catt identified women according to their professional occupations as if belonging to high status groups made these women particularly fit voters.

> Behold him [Uncle Sam] again, welcoming the boys of twenty-one and the newly-made immigrant citizen to "a voice in their own government" while he denies the fundamental right of democracy to thousands of women public school teachers . . . , to women college presidents, to women who preach in our pulpits, interpret law in our courts, preside over our hospitals, write books and magazines and serve in every uplifting moral and social enterprise.[34]

In some of her speeches Stanton also focused exclusively on women from elite groups as potential voters. She demanded suffrage for women ministers, lawyers, literary figures, scientists and teachers, without mention of maids, shop girls, and sweatshop seamstresses.

In addition to their professional skills, Stanton focused on culture and refinement as attributes making women worthy voters. Since few women from the lower class had an opportunity to develop refinement, Stanton's appeal was an appeal on behalf of middle- and upper-class women; it was intolerable that women of such culture and refinement should be ruled by ignorant, uncouth men from the lower classes.

------

[32]*Proceedings of the First Anniversary of the American Equal Rights Association* (New York: Robert J. Johnston, 1867) 15.

[33]Carrie Chapman, Catt, *An Address to the Congress of the United States* (New York: National Woman Suffrage Publishing Company, n.d.) 19.

[34]Ibid., 2.

It is sufficiently humiliating to a proud woman to be reminded ever and anon in the polite world that she's a political nonentity; to have the fact gracefully mourned over, or wittily laughed at, in classic words and cultured voice by one's superior in knowledge, wisdom, and power; but to hear the rights of women scorned in foreign tongue and native gibberish by everything in manhood's form is enough to fire the soul of those who think and feel.[35]

Allusions to culture and refinement, along with mentions of professional skills, show that Stanton and Catt were particularly concerned about the enfranchisement of upper-class women. That such women should be subject to their social and educational inferiors was as objectionable as being ruled by their racial inferiors.

Motivations and Contradictions

Resentment of Inferiors

All three suffrage leaders revealed resentment that men from inferior racial and social groups could vote while the nation's best women could not. The wellsprings of racist, nativist, and class arguments were strong emotions. These women felt humiliated and degraded because the nation ignored their pleas for suffrage while it reached out to crown with sovereignty those whom they deemed foreigners, savages, and ex-slaves. Catt predicted that women who were knowledgeable about history would always resent the fact that men fresh from slavery or steerage had been given the vote long before woman suffrage was permitted. Shaw spoke of the Fourteenth Amendment as "the most ungrateful and unjust act ever perpetrated by a republic" on women who were "reduced to the plane of subjects to enfranchised slaves." This was an "unspeakable degradation." The Dawes Act, which offered citizenship to Indians, caused the same bitterness. The strongest response came from Catt. "But in all time no insult was ever visited upon her [woman] which could compare with that of the American government which lifted out of savagery, half-barbarous Indians and made them the political rulers over the college bred, moral, intelligent women citizens."[36]

Nineteenth-century naturalization policies left native-born suffragists envious of the ease with which immigrant men could become voters. To Stanton, the political subjection of white, native-born women to foreign-

---

[35]Stanton, Anthony, and Gage, eds., *History of Woman Suffrage*, 2:334.

[36]Ida H. Harper, ed., *The History of Woman Suffrage* (New York: National American Woman Suffrage Association, 1922) 5:160; "Subject and Sovereign," Carrie Chapman Catt Papers, box 3, New York Public Library.

born men was "the most bitter drop in the cup of our grief."[37] Shaw repeatedly told audiences that "American" women were humiliated because they were governed by men of every nationality and race. She contrasted their position unfavorably with that of women in more homogeneous countries such as France or Germany, who were governed only by men sharing their own racial stock.

Catt summarized the frustration of white, native-born women who saw every class of men ushered to the seat of power before them.

> Whatever the outcome, the situation is one full of humiliation for American women. They have seen the negro freed from bondage and endowed with the suffrage, the Indian stopped in his murderous enterprises to be enfranchised, and now the force of our mighty nation is to enfranchise these unknown and untested Americans.[38]

The unknown and untested Americans to whom Catt alluded were those who had newly come under United States authority as a result of the Spanish-American War. White, native-born suffragists resented bitterly that such men participated in a government which still excluded Anglo-Saxon women.

Native-born, black suffragists were not immune from resentment toward the foreign-born who seemed to have easy access to rights denied native-born blacks. In 1894 an unsigned editorial in the black suffragist paper, *Woman's Era,* denounced supporters of a plan to deport blacks to Africa involuntarily. The writer expressed bitterness over foreign-born support for the deportation plan.

> The audacity of foreigners who flee their native land and seek refuge here but a day before they join in the hue and cry against native born citizens of this land is becoming intolerable. No government upon earth would permit it but the United States, and all the signs of the times point to a time not far off where self defence and self protection will force this government to protect its own people and to teach foreigners that this land is for Americans black or white and that other men are welccme [*sic*] and can come here only by behaving themselves and steering clear of plots and schemes against the people and the citizens who are here by right.

In her eloquent 1891 plea for Negro suggrage, Frances Ellen Watkins Harper voiced a negative, stereotypical view of immigrants as dangerous

---

[37]"The Degradation of Disfranchisement," Elizabeth Cady Stanton Papers, box 10, Library of Congress.

[38]Carrie Chapman Catt, "Our New Responsibilities," *Woman's Journal,* 1 October 1898, 317.

troublemakers. She insisted that blacks were not among the dynamite carrying, red banner waving anarchists threatening the nation. Blacks were loyal to the American flag. In return, the government should guarantee that "every *American-born* child shall be able to read upon its folds liberty for all and chains for none."[39]

When privileged, white, native-born suffragists used racial, ethnic, and class arguments, they found a release for feelings of humiliation occasioned by their subjugation to men whom they considered their inferiors. Nativist arguments also served as a means to lash out against those whom native-born suffragists held as partially responsible for their disfranchisement. These suffrage leaders viewed the opposition of foreign male voters as a chief factor in the loss of many state referendum campaigns. In her autobiography Shaw blamed the 1890 South Dakota defeat on foreign-born voters. She claimed that a district-by-district analysis of election results showed that heavy losses had occurred primarily in immigrant areas. In her review of the California battle in 1896 she alleged that all Chinese men had voted against woman suffrage. She offered no proof of this assertion beyond an anecdote about one Chinese cook who had reported to his mistress that "all Chinamen vote . . . no."[40] Catt's book on the suffrage struggle contained similar reflections. The history of defeat after defeat in state campaigns is punctuated with a common refrain. "It was the Russian's hour." "It was the hour of the foreigner in Oregon." "It was the hour of the Chinese."[41] By the turn of the century Stanton, too, had come to the conclusion that all foreigners were opposed to the enfranchisement of women. During this period she supported English-language literacy requirements for voters partially because they would decrease the number of foreigners opposing women at the polls.

Nativist arguments were likely to be comfortable for native-born women who perceived all foreign-born men as foes of woman suffrage. But their perception was inaccurate, and some woman suffrage leaders knew it. In testimony before the House Judiciary Committee Catt acknowledged that immigrant response to woman suffrage differed among the various ethnic groups. Russian Jews had supported woman suffrage, while Poles, Italians, and Germans were more often opposed. Analyzing a defeat suffered in Kansas, Stanton pointed out that the majority opposed to woman suffrage far exceeded the entire number of registered foreign-born voters. Even if none of the foreign-born men had voted, the

---

[39]"Difficulties of Colonization," *Woman's Era*, 24 March 1894, 9; Harper, "Duty to Dependent Races," 250 (emphasis added).

[40]Shaw, *Story of a Pioneer*, 274.

[41]Catt and Shuler, *Woman Suffrage and Politics*, 117, 123, 126.

votes of native-born men opposed to woman suffrage would have defeated the amendment.[42]

Universalizing Tendencies

Stanton, Catt, and Shaw all had extensive international contacts that yielded contradictions of their nativist assertions.[43] All three suffragists traveled abroad and lectured to international suffrage gatherings both in the United States and in Europe. In remarks before such international suffrage groups they were likely to make statements inconsistent with the nativist arguments they sometimes offered before American audiences. At such gatherings the suffragists alluded to a common experience shared by women as women without regard to their racial or ethnic origin. In Stanton's words, all women faced "the artificial distinctions of sex," giving rise to a "universal [female] sense of injustice, that forms a common bond of union between them." Catt, too, believed that the experience of sexual discrimination was shared by women of many nations. That shared suffering created a "solidarity of a sex."[44] Such assertions of sexual solidarity hardly squared with the claim that Anglo-Saxon women would join their own men to outvote women from other ethnic groups.

Not only did suffragists allude to a common female experience of oppression that bonded together women of varying nationalities; they also insisted that there were lessons to be learned from women of other nations. Stanton predicted that contact with such women would encourage American women to broaden their interests, liberalize their opinions, and sharpen their concern for the good of mankind. Shaw further predicted that international suffrage meetings would "show us that those who speak English are not the only ones whose hearts are alive to the great flame of liberty."[45] Claims that feminists from other nations had much to teach Americans about open-mindedness and the love of liberty clashed with the

---

[42]"Statement of Mrs. Carrie Chapman Catt of New York Before the Committee of the Judiciary, House of Representatives of the United States," Carrie Chapman Catt Papers, box 3, New York Public Library; Elizabeth Cady Stanton, "Educated Suffrage and Hope," *Woman's Journal*, 8 December 1894, 385.

[43]Shaw and Stanton also had personal experiences that broadened their outlook. Shaw was a foreign-born citizen; her parents brought her to the United States at the age of five. Stanton had one child who married a French citizen and one who married a British citizen. Catt was a leader of the International Woman Suffrage Alliance from its inception in 1904 until 1923.

[44]"Address of Welcome to the International Council of Women," Elizabeth Cady Stanton Papers, box 10, Library of Congress; Carrie Chapman Catt, *Mrs. Catt's International Address* (Warren OH: National Woman Suffrage Association, n.d.) 8.

[45]"Address of Welcome to the International Council of Women," Elizabeth Cady Stanton Papers, box 10, Library of Congress; Linkugel, "Speeches of Shaw," 2:412.

argument that foreigners were incapable of comprehending the genius of American free institutions and therefore ought to be outvoted by native-born American women.

A 1917 query from *The Crisis*, the magazine of the NAACP, provided another occasion for Shaw and Catt to take positions at odds with their more racist and nativist statements. *The Crisis* editor W. E. B. DuBois had given three prominent suffragists an opportunity to appeal to black voters in the issue released just before the 1917 woman suffrage referendum in New York State. Their remarks appeared under the title, "The Colored American and Suffrage." Shaw summarized her position succinctly. "I have never been able, and doubtless never shall be able to understand why one citizen who contributes to the support of the Government, and who is submissive to its authority, should have any more right than any other citizen, under like conditions, to free access to the ballot box."[46] Shaw firmly reiterated her stance that any productive, law-abiding citizen has an equal right to a say in the government.

The article in *The Crisis* was by no means the only place where Shaw took that stand. She maintained the same position when questioned by proponents of legislation designed to restrict immigrant suffrage. Any man, foreign-born or native-born, who contributed his labor to the building of America was, in Shaw's opinion, entitled to vote. "I am democratic enough to believe it is right for all men who put into the life of this nation their strength, their energy, their brawn and brain; who rear and educate their children, to have a voice in their government." While she believed that men from all groups have a right to a voice in the government, Shaw was frustrated that less qualified men—such as immigrants, blacks, and Indians—had the ballot, while well-qualified Anglo-Saxon women did not. Her solution was not to limit male suffrage, but immediately to enfranchise all women. Then the time might truly come when "there will be no such thing as a Colored American, any more than a German-American or an Irish-American or any other kind of American, except a plain American Citizen."[47]

Catt's understanding of democracy provided the theme of her reflection on Negro suffrage. "Everybody counts in applying democracy. And there will never be a true democracy until every responsible and law-abiding adult in it, without regard to race, sex, color or creed has his or her own inalienable and unpurchasable voice in the government."[48] Catt believed that all qualified citizens, without regard to sex, race, or creed, were entitled to participate in government. While at times she spoke approv-

---

[46]"Votes for All: A Symposium," *The Crisis* 15 (November 1917): 19.

[47]Linkugel, "Speeches of Shaw," 2:613-14; "Votes for All," 19.

[48]"Votes for All," 20.

ingly of literacy or property requirements for voters, she insisted that such tests must be administered evenhandedly. She condemned literacy tests devised to exclude adequately educated blacks, while permitting illiterate whites to vote.

Woman suffrage was but one aspect of the struggle for that universal democracy that was Catt's theme. She reminded blacks that suffragists were fighting for equal rights for all women, black as well as white. "For just as the world war is no white man's war, but every man's war, so is the struggle for woman suffrage no white woman's struggle, but every woman's struggle."[49]

Catt's awareness of the injustices suffered by blacks was manifest in her response to *The Crisis*. She expressed horror at mob violence against blacks in East St. Louis, Illinois, and she was distressed to hear that fellow suffragists who had been arrested for picketing the White House indulged in a "retrograde outburst" of protest when housed with black prisoners. She put her faith in true democracy as the best arena in which to battle such evils and asked that women receive the suffrage as their weapon in the struggle.

Catt also expressed concern about racism and nativism when she listened to a speech on woman suffrage and the South at the 1903 NAWSA convention. A speaker from Mississippi predicted that Northern Anglo-Saxon women, threatened by an influx of inferior immigrants, would look to the South for means to preserve Anglo-Saxon supremacy, whereupon Southern white women would gladly reveal the connection between woman suffrage and Anglo-Saxon political dominance. In remarks following the speech Catt cautioned against excessive pride in one's Anglo-Saxon origin.

> We are all of us apt to be arrogant on the score of our Anglo-Saxon blood, but we must remember that ages ago the ancestors of the Anglo-Saxons were regarded as so low and embruted that the Romans refused to have them for slaves. The race that will be dominant through the ages will be the one that proves itself the most worthy.[50]

"Woman Versus the Indian"

White suffrage leaders like Stanton, Shaw, and Catt contradicted themselves when they mixed racist and nativist arguments with assertions that all adult citizens have a right to participate in the government under which they live. Black suffragist Anna Julia Cooper exposed this contradiction in an essay entitled, "Woman Versus the Indian." Cooper took her

---

[49]Ibid.

[50]Harper, ed., *History of Woman Suffrage*, 5:83.

title from the title of a speech by Anna Howard Shaw. Cooper acknowledged, "That Miss Shaw is broad and just and liberal in principal [*sic*] is proved beyond contradiction. Her noble generosity and womanly firmness are unimpeachable." Nonetheless, Cooper objected strenuously to promoting white, privileged women's rights through the use of comparisons which denigrated the other socially disadvantaged groups. "Woman should not, even by inference, or for the sake of argument, seem to disparage what is weak." She bitterly denounced racist talk as unworthy of the women's movement.[51]

When Cooper paraphrased the racist arguments used by white suffragists, their seaminess was even more obvious.

> The great burly black man, ignorant and gross and depraved, is allowed to vote; while the franchise is withheld from the intelligent and refined, the pure-minded and lofty souled white woman. Even the untamed and untamable Indian of the prairie, who can answer nothing but 'ugh' to great economic and civic questions is thought by some worthy to wield the ballot which is still denied the Puritan maid and the first lady of Virginia.

Cooper called such arguments a travesty of the real case for woman suffrage. "Why should woman become plaintiff in a suit versus the Indian, or the Negro or any other race or class who have been crushed under the iron heel of Anglo-Saxon power and selfishness?"[52] Cooper contended that arguments that pit one deprived group against another ignore the critical fact that movements on behalf of such groups are all linked. In her opinion, it is always a mistake when leaders of a movement for greater social justice allow themselves to be blinded by some narrow consideration of their own group's immediate interests. There can be no *real* advantage to be gained for one group at the expense of the others. "For woman's cause is the cause of the weak; and when all the weak shall have received their due consideration, then woman will have her 'rights,' and the Indian will have his rights, and the Negro will have his rights."[53]

Cooper conceded that the solidarity with the weak that she demanded of leaders of the women's movement would not be easy to attain. Such principled action would require "a determined front and a courageous, unwavering, stalwart heart." She understood the pressures that racist Southern white women were exerting on woman suffrage leaders, and she sympathized with white suffrage leaders caught between the Southern "lady" and black women, but she insisted that the real significance of the

---

[51]Cooper, *Voice from the South*, 80, 117.

[52]Ibid., 123.

[53]Ibid., 117.

women's movement was in its drive for universal human rights. The women's movement must recognize its links to other movements to end other forms of human oppression. Otherwise, the women's movement degenerates into a useless "blue stocking debate or an aristocratic pink tea."[54]

Absence of Divine Blessing

While Stanton, Shaw, and Catt blatantly manipulated the myth of Anglo-Saxon supremacy all too often, they never offered theological justifications for their appeals to the Anglo-Saxon mystique. This is not to say that it is difficult to connect Anglo-Saxon supremacy to religious ideas. Other late nineteenth-century writers were certainly able to make that connection. Representative of this latter group was Josiah Strong, author of the popular work, *Our Country*.

Strong was willing to assign Anglo-Saxons as an ethnic group a crucial role in an evolutionary process under the direct guidance of God. According to him, God was grooming American Anglo-Saxons for the task of spreading both Protestant Christianity and democratic government throughout the world. "The Anglo-Saxon is the representative of two great ideas, which are closely related. One of them is that of civil liberty. . . . The other . . . is that of a pure, *spiritual* Christianity."[55] Strong considered it inevitable that the Protestant Reformation with its emphasis on the right of personal conscience should have arisen among a Teutonic people—the Germans—not a Latin people. The Teutonic race, with Anglo-Saxon Americans at its pinnacle, was a freedom-loving people. This ethnic group had, therefore, developed the mechanisms of self-government. The Anglo-Saxons, as the guardians of both pure Christianity and democracy, were divinely commissioned to spread these ideals among the lesser peoples of the earth.

The immense natural resources of the American continent, its bracing climate, its contiguous stretch of fertile land, and its ingenious labor force were all resources which the deity had provided to strengthen American Anglo-Saxons for their task of spreading the highest form of Christian civilization throughout the world during the twentieth century. If Americans could mobilize to combat the internal threats to Anglo-Saxon civilization posed by immigration, Roman Catholicism, Mormonism, socialism, the liquor interests, and urbanization, then American Anglo-Saxons would stand on the verge of the final age of history when the Anglo-Saxon race, "representative . . . of the largest liberty, the highest civilization—having

---

[54]Ibid., 100, 123.

[55]Josiah Strong, *Our Country: Its Possible Future and Its Present Crisis* (New York: American Home Missionary Society, 1885) 159-60.

developed peculiarly aggressive traits calculated to impress its institutions upon mankind, . . . [would] spread itself over the earth."[56]

Although Strong and others like him were willing to state bluntly that God had a special mission for Americans of Anglo-Saxon descent, Stanton, Catt, and Shaw never gave Anglo-Saxons any special divine blessing. They appealed to no theological ideals when invoking the Anglo-Saxon mystique.

In the last quarter of the nineteenth century, the myth of Anglo-Saxon superiority was a powerful social ideology. In this increasingly racist climate, white suffragists sometimes argued that woman suffrage would further strengthen Anglo-Saxon political dominance. They described Anglo-Saxon women as better acquainted with democratic principles and practices and as less easily corrupted by machine politicians. Some black suffragists asserted that black women would be less easily corrupted than black men. Nevertheless, black feminists defended the black race against the charge that its vote was purchasable.

White, native-born suffragists described blacks, native Americans, and immigrants as innately inferior beings. Such assertions were rooted in the resentment that upper-class, native-born, white women felt when they saw their "inferiors" vote, while they could not. While religion could have been used to legitimate race and ethnic prejudice, Stanton, Shaw, and Catt refrained from giving Anglo-Saxon superiority divine blessing.

As Anna Julia Cooper powerfully demonstrated, appeals to the Anglo-Saxon mystique imperilled the moral legitimacy of the woman suffrage movement, which at is best struggled to gain full citizenship for all women. Many of the white suffragist appeals to the myth of True Womanhood entrapped these women in a more subtle version of the same contradiction—fighting for the rights of all women by using arguments that demeaned socially vulnerable women.

---

[56]Ibid., 175.

3 | The True Woman

WHITE FEMINISTS openly manipulated white supremacist ideology in order to persuade Anglo-Saxon men to share political power with Anglo-Saxon women. They appealed to a more subtle form of race and class prejudice when they invoked the American myth of True Womanhood.

Opinion molders in nineteenth-century America pictured woman as a purer, higher being devoted to home, husband, and children. This image of woman was, of course, at variance with the experience of many women of the period. The True Woman was almost certainly the wife of a well-to-do male (usually white and native-born) whose economic success made it possible for her to reign as queen of the home. Poor women, black women, and immigrant women often led lives that precluded the development of a "refined," "feminine" character.

Anti-suffragists charged that the sordid political realm was no environment for the True Woman. Gradually, however, suffragists began to claim that the True Woman armed with the ballot was the very person best able to clean up American politics. While black feminists struggled to expand the ideal of True Womanhood to encompass their life experiences, white suffragists played on a narrow version of this social ideal in order to persuade privileged white men that their sisters, mothers, and wives should have the ballot.

The Nineteenth-Century Ideal of Womanhood

In nineteenth-century America there was a social consensus about the True Woman's chief virtues. "The nineteenth century was confident that it knew the differences between the sexes and that these differences were total and innate. Women were inherently more religious, modest, passive and domestic."[1] Women were also nurturing, pure, sweetly persuasive, and self-sacrificing.

Industrialization in the nineteenth century in the United States transformed women's experience. The site of productive labor moved from the farm or workshop-home to the factory. When men began leaving home to work in factories and offices, comfortably situated middle-class married

---

[1]Barbara Welter, *Dimity Convictions: The American Woman in the Nineteenth Century* (Athens OH: Ohio University Press, 1976) 17.

women were left alone with their children. At the same time, female tasks such as cloth making and food processing were increasingly industrialized. Those women who were freed from these tasks had more time to devote to their children. As middle-class women lost other traditionally female duties, motherhood was expanded into a full-time occupation. An ideology extravagantly praising maternal love was developed to support this newly enlarged role. An example of the praise heaped on mothers was one journalist's statement that "a mother is, next to God, all powerful."[2] The black educator Anna Julia Cooper concurred. "Woman, Mother—your responsibility is one that might make angels tremble and fear to take hold. . . . [It is] the most sacred and solemn trust ever confided by God to human kind."[3]

Women were assured that their job in rearing the young was a vitally important one. The mother is the person who permanently shapes the moral character of her children. The author of *Letters to Mothers* exclaimed, "How entire and perfect is this dominion over the unformed character of your infant."[4] The self-forgetful, patient mother gains "ineradicable, inexpugnable possession of the life of sons and daughters," while the best a father obtains is "a certain power" and "dear respect."[5] A mother's moral sway had political as well as personal effects. Mothers could redeem the social order by raising highly moral sons, who would then transform the economic and political realms.

Nineteenth-century writers assumed that woman's biological ability to conceive and bear children was matched by a maternal instinct that especially suited her to rear them. Women were by nature best equipped to raise the nation's young. As teachers as well as mothers, women could mold the character of the future citizenry. As the nineteenth century progressed, women came to dominate the teaching profession. Local school boards liked women teachers because "they were cheap and submissive. . . . Paid 30 to 50 percent less than men, they showed endless patience with poor living conditions, overcrowded one-room schools, and inadequate teaching equipment."[6] Both those who wanted to expand women's em-

---

[2]*The Public Ledger and Daily Transcript*, quoted in Arthur W. Calhoun, *A Social History of the American Family*, 3 vols. (New York: Barnes & Noble, 1945) 2:84-85.

[3]Anna J. Cooper, *A Voice from the South* (Xenia OH: Aldine Printing House, 1892) 22.

[4]Lydia Huntley Sigourney, *Letters to Mothers*, quoted in Ann Douglas, *The Feminization of American Culture* (New York: Avon Books, 1977) 88.

[5]Horace Bushnell, *Women's Suffrage: The Reform Against Nature* (New York: Charles Scribner & Company, 1869) 171.

[6]Barbara Mayer Wertheimer, *We Were There: The Story of Working Women in America* (New York: Pantheon Books, 1977) 160.

ployment options and those who wanted to exploit women as cheap educational laborers described women as uniquely suited for the education of young children. Catherine Beecher, a nineteenth-century authority on education, told Americans, "It is woman who is the natural and appropriate guardian of childhood. It is woman who has those tender sympathies which can most readily feel for the wants and sufferings of the young."[7]

Woman's sublime influence was not restricted to children, however. She could hope to influence the public behavior of adult males as well. Beecher dedicated *The American Woman's Home* "to the women of America, in whose hands rest the real destinies of the republic. . . . "[8] American women not only shaped their sons into upright, patriotic citizens, but also preserved the rectitude of adult male relatives through the sweeter, higher influence that women exercised in the home.

Home, now divorced from many economically productive functions, became a place of refuge from the cutthroat competition of the marketplace. Woman, preserved from the taint of business and politics, could embody those values of compassion and self-sacrifice that man was forced to eschew. In the words of one New England minister, "It is at home, where man . . . seeks a refuge from the vexations and embarrassments of business, . . . where some of his finest sympathies, tastes, and moral and religious feelings are formed and nourished;—where is the treasury of pure disinterested love, such as is seldom found in the busy walks of a selfish and calculating world."[9] Nineteenth-century proponents of True Womanhood hoped that women, who safeguarded esteemed (but seemingly impractical) moral and religious values, would guarantee that these endangered values would not completely disappear from American society.

Women were urged to use their charms to persuade male relatives to go forth from the home to do right.

> Woman is to win every thing by peace and love; by making herself so much respected, esteemed and loved, that to yield to her opinions and to gratify her wishes, will be the free will offering of the heart. But this is to be all accomplished in the domestic and social circle. There let every woman become so cultivated and refined in intellect . . . so benevolent in feeling and action . . . so unassuming and unambitious . . . as that every heart will repose in her pres-

---

[7]Catherine Esther Beecher, *The Duty of American Women to Their Country* (New York: Harper & Brothers, 1845) 65.

[8]Catherine E. Beecher and Harriet Beecher Stowe, *The American Woman's Home* (New York: J. B. Ford and Co., 1869) frontispiece.

[9]Quoted in Nancy F. Cott, *The Bonds of Womanhood: "Woman's Sphere" in New England, 1780-1835* (New Haven: Yale University Press, 1977) 64.

ence; then, the fathers, the husbands, and the sons, will find an influence thrown around them, to which they will yield not only
willingly but proudly.[10]

Admirers insisted that women's soft persuasion could be highly effective,
but if women became direct and assertive, their vital influence would be
lost. Women needed to maintain their sweet persuasiveness in order to
draw men up to their own high moral plane, for women were more virtuous than men. When nineteenth-century writers praised the virtues of
women, they had in mind *private* virtues. Virtue in the female meant sexual purity and temperance, not courage or justice. "Purity, modesty, and
lack of passion were among the most valued of the qualities generally attributed to women. Since men were viewed as naturally lustful and aggressive, women's reticence seemed to serve as the principal defense of
moral standards."[11]

Women were also said to be more religious than men. In terms of
church membership, this was certainly true. Since the mid-seventeenth
century, female members had outnumbered males in the churches.[12]
Flourishing, female, church-related, voluntary associations were among
the few social outlets acceptable for a virtuous woman in antebellum
America. Women were said to have a greater receptivity to spiritual influences. The theologian Horace Bushnell held a typical belief that women's
"moral nature is more delicately perceptive. Their religious inspirations,
or inspirabilities, put them closer to God."[13] Woman's sheltered life in the
home was seen as a shield against corruption by mercenary temptations
or worldly allures. The religious woman could in turn transmit values of
purity, compassion, and piety to others—especially to children under her
care. Therefore, ironically, "the ideal woman . . . was to exert moral [and
religious] pressure on a society in whose operations she had little part."[14]

Woman's Contributions to Good Government

Homemaking Skills

While many nineteenth-century writers claimed that woman was a
purer being who should exercise moral power in the shelter of the home,

---

[10]Catherine E. Beecher, *An Essay on Slavery and Abolitionism, with Reference to the Duty of American Females*, 2d ed. (Boston: Parkins and Marvin, 1836) 100.

[11]Robert W. Smuts, *Women and Work in America* (New York: Columbia University Press, 1959) 117.

[12]Cott, *Bonds of Womanhood*, 126; Douglas, *Feminization of American Culture*, 116-
17.

[13]Bushnell, *Women's Suffrage*, 57.

[14]Douglas, *Feminization of American Culture*, 69.

feminists turned that argument on its head. Woman *is*, they agreed, a purer being with special responsibilities to her loved ones, but that requires her to clean up the society in which her family lives. Given late nineteenth-century political corruption, government seemed to need a thorough housecleaning, and who better to supervise it than those best acquainted with housecleaning—American homemakers. Since government performed a number of functions that can be described as housekeeping on a massive scale, the involvement of women in the affairs of state would be advantageous. Catt identified the similarity between government tasks and homemaking tasks.

> City garbage collection is seen quickly to be a multiplication of many house garbage cans. City markets mean that the places where the individual housewife buys her children's food are multiplied many times over. Police systems mean to her the safeguarding of the streets on which her children walk. The woman, more intimately even than the man, finds government a matter related to her own work at every turn.[15]

Insofar as the government concerned itself with functions that women well understood, such as the maintenance of healthful, sanitary living conditions, women were admirably equipped to render judgment on government at the polls.

Sensitive to concerns of health and sanitation, women voters would demand adequate services in these areas. Men, who were less acquainted with such aspects of life, were more likely to tolerate municipal neglect. Shaw contended that the women who nursed children during epidemics of scarlet fever and diphtheria would not tolerate impure water, uninspected milk, and inadequate sewage systems. Catt declared that no good housekeeper would have permitted rodents to consume much needed wartime food supplies. Only male insensitivity and female powerlessness permitted such waste. Catt even claimed that where women did have the vote, public health and welfare questions were better handled than in areas where women were disfranchised.[16]

If woman's housekeeping experience made her a voter sensitive to issues of public health and sanitation, her child-rearing experience made

---

[15]Carrie Chapman Catt, "Ready for Citizenship," *The Public: An International Journal of Fundamental Democracy* 20 (24 August 1917): 818.

[16]Wilmer A. Linkugel, "The Speeches of Anna Howard Shaw: Collected and Edited with Introduction and Notes," 2 vols. (Ph.D. diss., University of Wisconsin, 1961) 2:449-51; "Mrs. Catt at the State Suffrage Conference in Saratoga, NY," Carrie Chapman Catt Papers, box 3, Astor, Lenox, and Tilden Foundations, Rare Books and Manuscripts Division, New York Public Library; *Do You Know?* (New York: National American Woman Suffrage Association, 1914) 9-10.

her alert to child welfare issues. Catt, aware of women's heavy responsibilities for child care, argued that women were best suited by experience to vote on public policies affecting home and children. When public education and public recreation facilities were under discussion, women's voices needed to be heard. Such public concerns were often neglected because "men have neither opportunity nor inclination to understand and defend the crying demands of the home, women, and children for political care."[17]

Black suffragist Coralee Franklin Cook believed that the experience of childbirth opened up woman's heart to the needs of all children. She told readers of *The Crisis*, "The woman who smilingly goes out, willing to meet the Death Angel, that a child may be born, comes back from that journey, not only the mother of her own babe, but a near-mother to all other children."[18] Cook thought that women sensitized by childbearing would use the ballot to support public policies benefiting children.

Stanton contended that woman's child-rearing experience made her sensitive not only to questions affecting children, but also to policies affecting any disadvantaged group. Within the family, good mothers learned to treat each child fairly—giving each equal opportunity for growth. If one child were handicapped, the mother would offer that child the extra assistance he or she needed for a full life. If women with this mothering instinct were brought into the larger society, they would demand the same equal justice for all citizens in the republic that they demanded for all children at home. Stanton believed that women would hold the government to what she saw as its true objective—to protect the weak against the strong.[19]

Suffragists also inverted the argument that mothers would make good voters, claiming that female voters would be good mothers. They asserted that women needed political power in order to perform effectively in their role as child rearers. Since children were formed by influences from the total society as well as by influences within the home, women could not shape the characters of their children unless they possessed some control over social conditions. Stanton exhorted mothers to demand that political control. Horrified by mob violence against antislavery speakers, she insisted that women must involve themselves in community affairs. "When I look around and see brave, strong, full grown men swamped in the whirlpool of numbers, I feel that a mother's duty is not all at home. Love

---

[17]Letter to the *New York Times*, Carrie Chapman Catt Papers, box 5, New York Public Library.

[18]Coralee Franklin Cook, "Votes for Mothers," *The Crisis*, August 1915, 84.

[19]"Butterflies of Fashion," Elizabeth Cady Stanton Papers, box 3, Library of Congress, Washington DC.

prompts us to clear up the rubbish in the outer world, and pluck the thorns from the paths our sons so soon must tread."[20]

Shaw offered several examples of specific social conditions that excited the interest of mothers. Mothers were vitally concerned about the regulation of child labor, liquor, and gambling. Social permissiveness in any of these areas threatened to destroy the young lives that mothers had carefully nurtured. In the case of both child labor and liquor, powerful industrial groups benefited from minimal government regulation. If women were to secure tighter controls to protect their children, they would need the ballot as a means of direct political influence. Shaw concluded one temperance lecture,

> Remember: the distiller is armed with a ballot; the brewer is armed with a ballot; the saloon-keeper is armed with a ballot; the bartender is armed with a ballot; the drunkard—is armed with a ballot. The home-maker, the child rearer, is powerless against such a foe without the ballot which determines political conditions, which influence public opinions and regulate social conditions in this country.[21]

The astute mother should perceive the ballot as necessary equipment for good child rearing.

Peace

Elizabeth Cady Stanton believed that women would support political decisions that safeguarded human life. She asserted that women had a unique understanding of the value of life because they suffered while bringing it into the world. Yet women's animosity to violence went deeper than a reverence for life occasioned by the birthing of a child. Stanton came, later in her life, to a belief in subtle, natural differences between the male and female character. According to Stanton, men were stern and aggressive—easily given to use of force. She informed a suffrage conference, "The male element is a destructive force, stern, selfish, aggrandizing, loving war, violence, conquest, acquisition, breeding in the material and moral world alike discord, disorder, disease and death."[22] The vices to which men were prone—cruelty and violence—could be eliminated from

---

[20]Elizabeth Cady Stanton, *Free Speech* (n.p., 1861) 1.

[21]Linkugel, "Speeches of Shaw," 2:843.

[22]Elizabeth Cady Stanton, Susan B. Anthony, and Mathilda J. Gage, eds., *The History of Woman Suffrage* (New York: Fowler and Wells, 1882) 2:351. Stanton clearly stated that her generalization about the male character did not apply to each and every man. Certain men, as individuals, demonstrated a much more balanced attitude toward life. However, these men were merely splendid exceptions; the majority of men, she thought, displayed the destructive characteristics she named.

the political arena if women possessing complementary virtues—compassion and respect for life—shared political power.

Stanton believed that women were by nature more sympathetic toward others and more concerned about the conservation and enhancement of life. As voters, women would demand government policies that would protect human life. Stanton's perception that women were the special guardians of life was the foundation for her belief that women with social power would explore all alternatives to war for the settlement of national and international disputes. She also thought that women would manifest their respect for life through political demands for humane prisons and mental hospitals and tough transportation safety regulations.[23]

Black suffragist Fannie Barrier Williams shared Stanton's assumption that women had a unique tenderness of heart that would give rise to more humane social policies. In a column for *Woman's Era*, Williams insisted that correctional facilities for young offenders were not run as they ought to be because "man alone has been the stern master." Williams believed that women possessed that "warmer heart and finer instincts for home training" that would be an invaluable resource in establishing a plan to find homes for "every dependent child susceptible to tender influence."[24]

Elizabeth Cady Stanton's regard for woman's peace-loving instincts led to her belief that the bloodshed of the Civil War could have been prevented if women in the North and South had shared in the political decision-making process.[25] Shaw shared Stanton's optimism about women's ability to prevent warfare. She asserted that the women of Europe might have averted World War I if they had had political power. Shaw agreed with Stanton's conviction that women have a peace-keeping bias related to their maternal experiences. Women risked their lives bringing children into the world, and they devoted years to raising those children at great personal cost. Speaking of the sacrifices a woman makes in rearing a son, Shaw said, "And then she did what no man has ever been asked to do, no father, she laid aside all her own aspirations for herself, her hopes, her ambitions, all aside that she might build herself into that tiny bit of life, that he might become a man."[26] Women having thus sacrificed would never give political assent to the slaughter of their sons.

---

[23]See, for example, "Prisons and Punishments," *The Revolution*, 7 January 1869, 9; "Our Jails and Prisons," *The Revolution*, 23 July 1868, 40; and "The Subjection of Woman," Elizabeth Cady Stanton Papers, box 3, Library of Congress.

[24]Fannie Barrier Williams, "The Need for Co-operation of Men and Women in Correctional Work," *Woman's Era*, May 1895, 4.

[25]Elizabeth Cady Stanton, "Rev. Joseph Thompson on Woman's Suffrage," *The Revolution*, 22 April 1869, 248.

[26]Linkugel, "Speeches of Shaw," 2:346.

Women deserved a say in questions of war and peace because they were the mothers of soldiers, but also because they were themselves the victims of war. With characteristic delicacy Shaw reminded her hearers of the sexual violence endured by women in war-torn countries. "You cannot read it because it is not printable; you cannot tell it because it is not speakable; you cannot even think it because it is not thinkable; the horrible crimes perpetrated against women by the blood drunken men of the war."[27] Women caught up in war face hunger, homelessness, their own death and that of their children. Therefore, the power to influence decisions of war and peace was vital to women.

It was also essential that women should have a voice in questions of war and peace because men had proved themselves incapable of judicious judgment in matters of war. In correspondence with the Dutch suffragist, Dr. Aletta Jacobs, Shaw expressed frustration with the male bureaucrats with whom she dealt in the course of her government service during World War I. "Men, I am convinced, never grow up and of all the animal creation are the least capable of reason." Men had set civilization on a destructive course. She hoped that the horrors of World War I would show them that woman's influence in government would be desirable. Catt agreed with Shaw that an exclusively male government is too contentious for the good of the nation or the world. "It has been made clear to me in the last few months that men are too belligerent to be trusted alone with governments. The world needs woman's restraining hand." Since men naturally favored war and women naturally favored peace, it was in the best interests of the nation that both sexes have effective voices in national policies. Anna Julia Cooper held a similar belief that men naturally strove for righteousness, while women innately promoted "its necessary 'other half,' " peace. Therefore, both women and men were needed to set social policies.[28]

Suffragists' claims that women were innately more peace loving and thus would, as voters, prevent war left them open to the contention of opponents that the ballot is a privilege reserved to those persons who have the obligation to fight in defense of the government. According to this theory, since peace-loving women are not fighters, they should not be voters. As the United States came closer and closer to entry into World War I, suffragists came under increasing pressure to prove that women were patriotic—that they would support wars in which the country was involved. The active participation of prominent woman suffrage leaders in

[27]Ibid., 290.

[28]Jane De Iongh, ed., *Letters from Dr. Anna Howard Shaw to Dr. Aletta Jacobs* (London: E. J. Brill, 1938) 124; Ida H. Harper, ed., *The History of Woman Suffrage* (New York: National American Woman Suffrage Association, 1922) 5:460; Cooper, *Voice from the South*, 57.

peace campaigns made the movement particularly vulnerable to such pressure.

As usual, Shaw met the objections of her opponents head on. Told that women could not fight, she described the brawls between women that she had witnessed as a young minister in Boston. "And when two women want to fight from the crowns of their heads to the soles of their feet they make a business of it. There are no rules regulating the art."[29] While Shaw's slum experience left her with no doubt that women were fully capable of all-out warfare, she still believed that the majority of women did not wish to fight.

While suffragists knew that women were capable of warlike behavior, they stressed more often women's contribution to war efforts from the home front. Wars were fought successfully because women undertook the myriad tasks necessary to sustain the army and civilians when men left for the front. "Without the work of women in field, factory and shop . . . without their production of food for the army and tax money to meet the enormous cost of war, any nation would come to an end, though its army were composed entirely of Alexanders and Napoleons."[30]

Shaw and Catt tried to reconcile their belief in woman's peace-loving instincts with their glorification of her role as war worker during World War I. They were helped by President Wilson's declaration that this war was the war to end all wars. In 1917 Catt insisted that the suffragists' war service was motivated by a desire to make future wars impossible. One day, she predicted, women would repudiate all war. Responding to opponents of woman suffrage who argued that since women cannot fight, they should not be allowed to vote, Catt replied,

> [Women] can fight, and have fought in wars and all down the centuries; but if they do go forth to fight, who shall keep the nation going? What is there to fight for? Thank God, they do not go to the front often! In the calm, sad moments at home they are learning to understand the wasteful cost of war as men have never done, and some day as one woman the motherhood of the world will refuse longer to give their sons to be shot in support of . . . false ideals of national honor.[31]

Virtue

Nineteenth-century Americans celebrated the moral qualities of women. Many white and black suffragists shared with their fellow Amer-

---

[29]Linkugel, "Speeches of Shaw," 2:883.

[30]"Women and War," Carrie Chapman Catt Papers, box 3, New York Public Library.

[31]Ibid.

icans the notion that women were naturally more virtuous than men. Since women were more virtuous, suffragists argued, woman suffrage would result in greater attention to moral values at the polls.

Suffragists contended that widening woman's sphere to include politics would increase the amount of compassion and sensitivity to others within the voter pool. Catt viewed women's social concern as distinctive. Women focused on human needs, while men concentrated on economic prosperity. "Women wanted to vote because the things which seemed to them most important, the welfare of human beings and the safety of human life, they saw neglected by men, especially in government."[32]

Black suffragist Anna Julia Cooper agreed that women brought a special perspective to social issues. Society at the end of the nineteenth century was like a child reared by a father alone. "It has needed the great mother heart to teach it to be pitiful, to love mercy, to succor the weak and care for the lowly." Of course, Cooper recognized that sometimes a compassionate man advocated social policies designed to protect the socially vulnerable, but she attributed this male sensitivity to the influence of the reformer's mother. Such a man was "simply materializing and giving back to the world in tangible form the ideal love and tenderness, devotion and care that have cherished and nourished the helpless period of his own existence."[33] Woman's sympathy was needed alongside man's rationality in the public realm.

Stanton proclaimed that women were more morally courageous because women had innate spiritual strength that men lacked. Women naturally held more strongly to moral principles than men did. The moral development of the human race was impeded because women lacked the social power to implement their ethical insights. Stanton occasionally connected male immorality with the dominance of gross sensuality in the male personality. If women were granted enlarged social responsibilities and opportunities, then women's higher spiritual attributes would balance men's lower appetites.[34]

The claim that women were more virtuous than men and that their voting would result in social betterment was difficult to substantiate. Suffragists attempted to prove their assertions by an appeal to numbers. More women than men were church members and charity workers; fewer women than men were criminals. Anna Howard Shaw claimed that women

---

[32]Untitled speech fragment, Carrie Chapman Catt Papers, box 11, Library of Congress, Washington DC.

[33]Cooper, *Voice from the South,* 51, 59-60.

[34]Speech to members of the National American Woman Suffrage Association, 1889, box 4; "The Subjection of Woman," box 3; and "The Family, the State, the Church," box 11, Elizabeth Cady Stanton Papers, Library of Congress.

comprised 75 percent of all church members and 90 percent of all charity workers. In a 1919 pamphlet Catt argued,

> Woman suffrage will increase the *moral vote*. Only one out of every twenty criminals are women. Women constitute a minority of drunkards and petty misdemeanants and in all the factors that tend to handicap the progress of society women form a minority; whereas in churches, schools and all organizations working for the uplift of humanity women are a majority.

Speaking of the black woman's religious contribution, black educator and suffragist, Nannie Helen Burroughs, declared, "The Negro Church means the Negro woman." She insisted that it was the labor and contributions of black women that sustained the vast majority of black churches.[35]

Such morally upright women would be especially desirable voters, for they would support public policies that encouraged virtue. Suffragists anticipated that women voters would support legislation to prohibit the sale of alcoholic drink, to curtail prostitution and the white slave trade, to end political corruption, and to ameliorate poverty.[36]

Motherheart of Woman, Motherheart of God

Suffragists claimed that women as women were needed at the polls. They felt that women as a group shared certain valuable personality traits. Some suffragists were willing to connect feminine virtues and the feminine attributes of God. Both Stanton and Shaw urged women to be proud that their femininity itself was a direct reflection of God. Stanton looked back to the account of creation in Genesis 1. God created man *and woman* in his/her likeness. Stanton took this to mean that both the masculine and the feminine element were blended in God. "If language has any meaning, we have in these texts a plain declaration of the existence of the feminine element in the Godhead, equal in power and glory with the masculine. The Heavenly Mother and Father!" Shaw agreed that there was a feminine and a masculine aspect to the divine. She personalized these

---

[35]Susan B. Anthony and Ida Husted Harper, eds., *The History of Woman Suffrage* (Rochester NY: Susan B. Anthony, 1902) 4:200; Carrie Chapman Catt, *Objections to the Federal Amendment* (New York: National Woman Suffrage Publishing Co., 1919) 27; N. H. Burroughs, "Black Women and Reform," *The Crisis*, August 1915, 87.

[36]While Catt maintained that women as voters would support significant social reforms, she rejected any simplistic notion that woman suffrage alone would wipe out social ills. Accused of having said that woman suffrage would mean the end of prostitution, she responded, "It is absurd to assume that . . . an evil which is the result of centuries of wrong conditions could be corrected by any one agency or in a brief period of time." "Mrs. Catt and Mr. Barry," *Woman's Journal*, 12 November 1910, 204.

forces, speaking of God as "the eternal parent of us all, the father and mother of the human soul." Shaw also asserted that both masculine and feminine traits could be observed in the character of Jesus.[37]

Shaw and Stanton seem to have drawn attention to the feminine aspect of the divine in order to give women a greater sense of worth. Once women accepted the motherhood of God, surely they would develop greater self-respect as women and would demand male recognition of their dignity. Shaw told women that if they suppressed their abilities in response to social pressure, they would hide "one-half of the divine nature" from the world's view.[38]

Shaw intimately connected God as loving mother and the motherly hearts of women. The love of a true mother is analogous to God's love. We long for God's succor as we would long to sit at the feet of our mothers. Indeed, when women act with maternal compassion, they are giving expression to God's love.[39]

Motherhood was, for Shaw, an important female experience. But she was concerned with motherhood as active care for others, not merely as physical childbearing. In some passages Shaw spoke of motherhood as the greatest service any citizen could render to the state. The mother is the one who enables the child to grow into a fit citizen. The true motherly heart stretches to concern itself with all of society's suffering ones.[40]

While Shaw saw a reflection of the divine in a mother's compassion, she knew the danger of characterizing women in one-dimensional terms. Real mothering is a very important act, but women are more than just mothers.[41] Since men are not reduced solely to the role of father, neither should women be limited to the role of mother. Shaw stated that one's own development as a person is more important even than the significant act of being a good mother. "The highest crown of glory that any woman can wear is pure, strong, noble, virtuous, dignified womanhood. After a woman has attained to that fullness of perfect womanhood, then let come to her what will, motherhood or spinsterhood, either will be equally with the other a crown of glory."[42]

In contrast to Shaw's analogy between the mother heart of woman and the motherly love of God, Stanton spoke of God as First Cause which set

---

[37]Elizabeth Cady Stanton et al., *The Woman's Bible* (New York: European Publishing Company, 1893) 1:14; Linkugel, "Speeches of Shaw," 2:57.

[38]Linkugel, "Speeches of Shaw," 2:57.

[39]Ibid.

[40]"If I Had a Vote," Dillon Collection, Shaw series, box 22, folder 489, Schlesinger Library, Radcliffe College, Cambridge MA.

[41]Linkugel, "Speeches of Shaw," 2:668.

[42]Ibid., 386.

the universe in motion and maintains it by unchanging laws. This First Cause dictated that there be an eternal balance between masculine and feminine. "The masculine and feminine elements, exactly equal, and balancing each other, are as essential to the maintenance of the equilibrium of the universe as positive and negative electricity, the centripetal and centrifugal forces, the laws of attraction which bind together all we know. . . . "[43]

Anna Julia Cooper shared a belief that the universe required a dynamic balance of masculine and feminine factors for its completeness and symmetry. She deplored the fact that women had been denied access to higher education, which was necessary to balance the masculine forces at work in the world with sorely needed complementary feminine influences.[44]

Stanton contended that nineteenth-century America was in such great difficulty because it had unjustly restricted woman's sphere and thus violated the balance of masculine and feminine that the order of the universe demanded. American society was experiencing growth in the material realm where the masculine was preeminent. "The world of trade and commerce, of material wealth, exploration, discovery, invention, belongs specifically to man and we can look with pride and thankfulness on the wonders he has achieved in the last half century."[45] Man had fulfilled his duties marvelously. Witness such wonders as transcontinental trains, great bridges, practical applications for electricity, or the telephone. Unfortunately, man had hampered woman from fulfilling her divinely ordained duties in the spiritual realm of life. "The question is often asked why it is that the moral and spiritual progress of the race does not keep pace with its intellectual and material achievements. I would answer, the moral and spiritual world belongs specifically to woman, and she is not yet awake to her duty in this realm of thought and action."[46]

Stanton agreed with antisuffragists that the deity had assigned man and woman responsibility for different realms, but she disagreed with them about the definition of those realms. Antisuffragists defined woman's realm in terms of place. A woman's place was in the home (and by extension in those places devoted to culture, religion, and private charity). A man's place was everywhere else—the legislature, the marketplace, and so forth. Stanton insisted that men and women must strive together in all these places. She defined woman's realm in terms of concern. In the home,

---

[43]Stanton et al., *The Woman's Bible*, 1:14.

[44]Cooper, *Voice from the South*, 57-60.

[45]Elizabeth Cady Staton, "Woman's Duty to Vote," *Woman's Tribune*, 15 December 1898, 10.

[46]Ibid.

in the legislature, in the marketplace, woman would be concerned about the moral and spiritual dimensions of experience. Man would be concerned about the intellectual and material dimension. When men and women worked together throughout the world, then the divinely appointed balance of masculine and feminine would be reestablished to the benefit of all humanity.

True Womanhood and Racism

White Women's Accountability for Racism

There is a discomforting corollary to the proposition that the True Woman possesses inherently stronger moral qualities that are necessary for a just social order. By implication, then, if a social evil exists, it is because the True Woman has failed to exercise her power for the good. On several occasions, black suffragists drew this conclusion, then held white women accountable for racism.

Anna Julia Cooper emphasized the influence of privileged white women over those social courtesies that were a crucial sign of respect for persons in daily social life. Upper-class white women, she believed, were responsible for setting the tone for American manners and morals. Fearful of losing what Cooper termed "caste," upper-class white women dictated rigid social barriers that excluded black persons. The privileged white woman maintained unjust social customs as "the lesson which she instills into her children with their first baby breakfasts, the injunction she lays upon husband and lover with direst penalties attached."[47]

In her 1904 magazine essay, "Lynching from a Negro's Point of View," Mary Church Terrell held the mothers of slaveholding families responsible for the turn-of-the-century atrocities being perpetrated by their descendants. "It is too much to expect, perhaps, that the children of women who for generations looked upon the hardships and degradations of their sisters of a darker hue with few if any protests, should have mercy and compassion upon the children of that oppressed race now."[48]

Nonetheless, Terrell believed that the influence of Southern white women, if it could be aroused on behalf of the victims of lynching, could be a powerful social force. Southern white women might be a tremendous influence for law and order, "if they would arise *in the purity and power of their womanhood to implore their fathers, husbands and sons* no longer to stain their hands with the black man's blood!" In an unusually frank statement before a Memphis, Tennessee, conference of Southern white women, black educator Charlotte Hawkins Brown told the women that "the negro

---

[47]Cooper, *Voice from the South*, 87.

[48]Mary Church Terrell, "Lynching from a Negro's Point of View," Mary Church Terrell Papers, reel 21, Library of Congress, Washington DC.

women of the South lay everything that happens to the members of her race at the door of the Southern white woman." Brown insisted that lynching would be stopped if the white women would "take hold of the situation."[49]

Black suffragists who criticized white women for not using their moral influence as women to end racism sometimes had an exalted notion of (privileged) white women's social power. Anna Julia Cooper believed that, at least where morality was concerned, white men ceded authority to the women of their race. "However tenaciously men may guard some prerogatives, they are our willing slaves in the sphere which they have always conceded to be woman's. Here, no one dares demur when her fiat has gone forth." An anonymous editorial writer in the black suffragist paper, *Woman's Era,* also credited her white sisters with great power, describing "the almost boundless possibilities of the American *white* woman; . . . the especial consideration which she enjoys in this country, anything being possible to her except the *act* in voting, and her growing influence now almost unlimited." Since the writer thought that white women possessed almost unlimited power, she concluded that "little more than a word from a white woman" could put an end to many of the injustices and outrages suffered by black people.[50]

In these remarks black suffragists exaggerated the social power of white women. They failed to understand the real power dynamics in the white community. To the extent that white men did give more than lip service to the influence of the True Woman, her power existed in a narrowly circumscribed private realm. It certainly did not encompass the political and economic power that white women would have had to possess if they were to mount an effective campaign against racism *relying solely on their own resources.*

To the extent that white suffragists accepted the myth of True Womanhood themselves and perpetuated it in their rhetoric, they left themselves vulnerable to recriminations from black women who held them fully accountable for society's ills. The feminists who used the True Woman myth revised it by calling for women to use their greater moral sensitivities in the public realm to enhance public life. However, combating racism was not high on the social reform agenda of most white suffragists. The editorial writer for *Woman's Era* glimpsed this contradiction, insisting that morally upright white women should no longer remain passive in the face of racism. Calling upon white women to face boldly the race question,

[49]Ibid. (emphasis added); Charlotte Hawkins Brown, "Speaking Up for the Race at Memphis, Tennessee," in *Black Women in White America: A Documentary History,* ed. Gerda Lerner (New York: Vintage Books, 1972) 470.

[50]Cooper, *Voice from the South,* 87; "A Word to the AAW," *Woman's Era,* November 1894, 8.

she declared, "It is a question they can no longer evade."[51] Nevertheless, most white suffragists did have a deliberate policy of evasion where Southern racism was concerned.

The Black Woman as a True Woman

Many black suffragists held white women accountable for racial injustices, in part, because they accepted the notion that women were uniquely responsible for maintaining a high moral tone in society. Black women who accepted the myth of True Womanhood also believed that they had a special duty *as black women* to uplift their race and that the ballot would help them discharge this responsibility.

Many educated black women accepted the notion that women as mothers had a uniquely powerful influence over the lives of children. They declared that black mothers had a special responsibility to uplift the black race. According to Anna Julia Cooper, the black home was the foundation for all the achievements of the race, and it was the black mother who set the tone for the home. "The atmosphere of homes is no rarer and purer and sweeter than are the mothers in those homes."[52]

Mary Church Terrell told the delegates to the 1899 meeting of the National Association of Colored Women that "the purification of the home must be our first consideration and care. It is in the home, where woman is really queen, that she wields her influence with the most telling effect." While cautioning that more privileged black women should not neglect their obligations to the poor, especially poor black children, she nonetheless declared, "in the mind and heart of every good and conscientious woman, the first place is occupied by home."[53]

Terrell described eloquently the plight of black mothers who realized that they must create in their children a character strong enough to resist the continuous assaults of racism. She pictured a black mother looking into the face of her newborn child. "She cannot thrill with joyful anticipations of the future [as a white mother can]. For before her babe she sees the thorny path of prejudice and proscription his little feet must tread." For Terrell the hope of the black race depended upon the ability of black women to "build the foundation of the next generation upon such a rock of morality, intelligence and strength, that the floods of proscription, prejudice and persecution may descend upon it in torrents and yet it will not be moved."[54]

---

[51]"A Word to the AAW," 8.

[52]Cooper, *Voice from the South*, 29.

[53]Mary Church Terrell, "The Duty of the National Association of Colored Women to the Race," Mary Church Terrell Papers, reel 20, Library of Congress.

[54]Ibid.; Paula Giddings, *When and Where I Enter: The Impact of Black Women on Race and Sex in America* (New York: William Morrow and Company, 1984) 100.

Since almost all black slaves had been forbidden to learn to read and write, there was a desperate need for teachers for black people after Emancipation. Even though black schools were segregated and poorly funded, they attracted many educated black women, because teaching was virtually the only profession open to them.[55] Many black educators believed that the women of their race had a special duty as teachers to mold black children into adults with morally upright characters. In 1899 black educator Lucy Craft Laney declared, "Women are by nature fitted for teaching very young children; their maternal instinct makes them patient and sympathetic with their charges." She continued, "in the kindergarten and primary school is the salvation of the race," because in these classrooms educated black women could instill in their pupils lessons of "cleanliness, truthfulness, loving kindness, love for nature, and love for Nature's God."[56]

Black suffragists argued that black mothers and teachers needed the ballot to protect the interests of black children. Concerned about inferior black schools, black suffragists asserted that enfranchised black women could force elected school boards to provide a better education for black children. Carrie W. Clifford, a black supporter of woman suffrage, proclaimed that the ballot was an important tool for black women, for "it is the ballot that opens the schoolhouse and closes the saloon."[57]

Black women took pride in their virtue—their moral purity. However, the white version of the myth of True Womanhood denied that black women were capable of sexual purity. The belief that black women were sexually promiscuous was so widespread in the late nineteenth century that Fannie Barrier Williams and Anna Julia Cooper felt obliged to meet the charge head-on when they addressed a largely white audience at the World's Congress of Representative Women in 1893. Williams prefaced her remarks with the regret that she had to address the topic, but she insisted that "the morality of our home life has been commented upon so disparagingly and meanly that we are placed in the unfortunate position of being defenders of our name."[58] Even privileged black women felt they were constantly challenged to defend themselves as pure, virtuous women.

[55]Mary Church Terrell described teaching as the only profession open to her. Moreover, she reported that in every city, the supply of black teachers exceeded the demand, because educated black women had so few other job opportunities. *A Colored Woman in a White World* (Washington DC: Randall, 1940) 386.

[56]Lucy Craft Laney, "The Burden of the Educated Colored Woman," in *Black Women in Nineteenth-Century American Life,* ed. Bert James Loewenberg and Ruth Bogin (University Park PA: Pennsylvania State University Press, 1976) 299-300.

[57]"Votes for Children," *The Crisis,* August 1915, 185.

[58]Fannie Barrier Williams, "The Intellectual Progress of the Colored Women of the United States Since Emancipation," in *Black Women in Nineteenth-Century American Life,* ed. Loewenberg and Bogin, 274.

Both Williams and Cooper charged that the moral purity of black women had been undermined by a slavery system that left black women unprotected in the face of sexual harassment and sexual violence from white men. Both women pointed with pride to the many black women who had resisted white male sexual assaults even at the risk of their own lives. Cooper declared,

> Yet all through the darkest period of the colored women's oppression in this country her yet unwritten history is full of heroic struggle, . . . that often ended in a horrible death, to maintain and protect that which woman holds dearer than life. The painful, patient, and silent toil of mothers to gain a fee simple title to the bodies of their daughters, the despairing fight, as of an entrapped tigress, to keep hallowed their own persons, would furnish material for epics.[59]

Cooper conceded that not all slave women had risked their lives to protect themselves against rape by white men. But no racial group, she continued, was composed entirely of heroines. Williams told her audience that in the thirty years since slavery had been abolished, freedwomen had striven hard to maintain their moral integrity and that of their daughters.

> The daughters of women who thirty years ago were not allowed to be modest, not allowed to follow the instincts of moral rectitude, who could cry for protection to no living man, have so elevated the moral tone of their social life that new and purer standards of personal worth have been created, and new ideals of womanhood, instinct with grace and delicacy, are everywhere recognized and emulated.[60]

Williams emphasized that many of those black women whose virtue had been compromised were the victims of continuing sexual harassment by white males. Black suffragists were particularly bitter about a vicious double standard distorting late nineteenth-century American life: virtuous black women were the unacknowledged victims of white rapists, while innocent black men were tortured and lynched ostensibly to protect white women's honor.

Black suffragists sometimes argued that the ballot would give black women a weapon with which to defend their purity. Enfranchised black women could put pressure on political leaders to pass legislation that would protect black women from sexual exploitation by white males. In partic-

[59]Quoted in *Black Women in Nineteenth-Century American Life*, ed. Loewenberg and Bogin, 329.

[60]Williams, "The Intellectual Progress of Colored Women," 275.

ular, black women sought to defeat or repeal antimiscegenation laws.[61] While many black women did not encourage interracial marriage, black women leaders tended to view antimiscegenation laws as legislation that allowed white men to escape responsibility for interracial sexual liaisons. The prominent black educator Nannie Helen Burroughs claimed that black women could use the ballot to get social protection against rapists. She complained, "when she [a black woman] appears in court in defence of her virtue, she is looked upon with amused contempt. She needs the ballot to reckon with men who place no value upon her virtue."[62]

While the ideal of the True Woman furnished a pattern of behavior for economically privileged white women, many whites doubted that the ideal was attainable by black women. The white woman who raised the mother of black educator Charlotte Hawkins Brown admonished her, "Caroline, if there be anything like a colored lady, I want you to be one." The white woman's words betray her doubt that there ever could be such a thing as a black lady. According to Anna Julia Cooper, these doubts were widely shared. She decried a "supercilious caste spirit in America which cynically assumes 'a Negro woman cannot be a lady.' "[63]

Historian Jacqueline Jones has shown that freedwomen who decided to stay home to care for their children and work in their own households rather than in the whites' fields were not praised for their devotion to home and motherhood. Instead, they were ridiculed as lazy and aspiring to a state in life beyond their due. "To apply the term 'lady-like' to a black woman was apparently the height of sarcasm; by socially prescribed definition, black women could never become 'ladies,' though they might display pretensions in that direction."[64]

If white suffragists had gone beyond facile generalizations about the virtues that woman would bring to the polls, they could have joined black suffragists in challenging the racist limitations of the myth of True Womanhood. But white suffragists were content to manipulate the myth of the True Woman for their own benefit without exploring how that myth related to the life experience of black women.

---

[61]Rosalyn Terborg-Penn, "Afro-Americans in the Struggle for Woman Suffrage" (Ann Arbor MI: University Microfilms, 1977) 227-34.

[62]Burroughs, "Black Women and Reform," 87.

[63]"Some Incidents in the Life and Career of Charlotte Hawkins Brown . . . ," Charlotte Hawkins Brown Papers, Schlesinger Library, Radcliffe College, Cambridge MA; Cooper, *Voice from the South*, 32.

[64]Jacqueline Jones, "Freed Women? Black Women, Work and the Family During the Civil War and Reconstruction," Working Paper #61, p. 27, Wellesley College Center for Research on Women, Wellesley MA.

4 | An Evaluation of the Suffragists' Arguments

APPEALS TO ANGLO-SAXON SUPERIORITY undercut the moral foundation for white women's suffrage. Suffragists claimed that all Americans shared a fundamental right as persons to participate in the political decisions that shaped their personal and corporate lives. Racist appeals and tactics are absolutely inconsistent with this belief. Appeals to the True Womanhood myth were often marred by more subtle race and class prejudice. Appeals to female superiority as well as racist appeals eviscerated the moral fiber of a movement that offered at its best a fresh vision of American society as a society in which all men *and women* are created equal and endowed with equal political rights. In order to evaluate suffragists' tactics and arguments fairly, it is necessary to place them within the specific political context in which they were used. White suffragists resorted to tacit cooperation with segregation practices and to racist and nativist claims in part because Southern support was essential for ratification of a woman suffrage amendment to the federal constitution.

The Necessity of Southern Support

Feminists tried several tactics to gain the vote for women. First, they attempted to convince Republicans to draft the Fourteenth and Fifteenth Amendments in universal terms. Thus, early in the Reconstruction period, some supporters of woman suffrage tried to secure the suffrage for black men and all women at the same time. But the Republicans refused to draft such a universal suffrage amendment, insisting that there was no general public support for woman suffrage. They feared that black male suffrage would be threatened by coupling it with the more controversial woman suffrage.

Republicans supported black male suffrage not only because it was morally right, but also because black men, grateful to the party of Lincoln for emancipation, were likely to vote Republican. White women, who constituted the bulk of women to benefit from woman suffrage, found it hard to persuade either political party to support their cause, because women were not likely to vote for a single party. Woman suffrage did not benefit Republicans in the same direct way that Negro suffrage did.

Second, suffrage leaders attempted to secure a Supreme Court decision declaring that women as citizens had a constitutionally guaranteed right to vote. This hope was dashed by the 1874 Supreme Court decision in the case of Minor vs. Happersett. In that case the justices declared unanimously that the United States Constitution does not guarantee suffrage to *any* citizen. Therefore, state laws restricting suffrage to men were not unconstitutional.

Third, woman suffrage leaders attempted to obtain the suffrage on a state by state basis. They tried to get state legislators to enfranchise women through legislative action. In a few states such as Wyoming, this was a successful tactic. But in some states the legislators refused to take direct action. In other states, where they were prohibited from enacting woman suffrage through legislation alone, voter referenda were held on the issue. According to Carrie Chapman Catt, suffragists engaged in 56 state woman suffrage campaigns, made 480 attempts to get state legislatures to pass state woman suffrage amendments, and petitioned 47 state constitutional conventions to enfranchise women. Most of these attempts were unsuccessful. By the turn of the century, after more than twenty-five years of effort, women had full suffrage in only four states—Wyoming, Utah, Colorado, and Idaho.[1]

Since state by state suffrage campaigns were so slow and so unproductive, astute suffrage leaders finally realized that a federal constitutional amendment was the only realistic means to secure the franchise for American women. Once women like Catt committed themselves to a federal constitutional amendment, they needed the support of some Southern states in order to ensure ratification. If thirteen states failed to ratify a proposed amendment, women would not be able to vote. Suffrage leaders considered Maryland, Mississippi, Louisiana, Florida, Kentucky, Tennessee, Virginia, North Carolina, South Carolina, Georgia, Alabama, and Delaware as Southern states. If these twelve held against woman suffrage, the loss of even one other state would defeat the amendment. Since a margin of one state was too slender, suffragists sought to crack the solid South. This refusal to write off the Southern states was vindicated when Tennessee became the final state to ratify the Nineteenth Amendment.

White suffragists began serious organizational work throughout the South about 1890. In the 1890s white Southerners were struggling to reestablish absolute dominance over blacks. Black men were being disfranchised in state after state, and stringent Jim Crow codes were being enacted.[2] The race question was the paramount social issue in the minds of Southerners during this period. Therefore, the most expedient way to

---

[1]Carrie Chapman Catt and Nettie R. Shuler, *Woman Suffrage and Politics* (1926; reprint ed., Seattle: University of Washington Press, 1969) 107; see also Eleanor Flexner, *Century of Struggle: The Woman's Rights Movement in the United States*, rev. ed. (Cambridge: Belknap Press of Harvard University Press, 1975) 178.

[2]See C. Vann Woodward, *The Strange Career of Jim Crow* (New York: Oxford University Press, 1974).

gain white, Southern support was to insist that woman suffrage in no way affected the social arrangements of the region. This was Shaw's point to her New Orleans questioner. Suffrage for women does not change the relationship of the races, for enfranchised or disfranchised, white and black women are political equals.

The race question bedeviled white woman suffrage leaders from their first serious efforts to organize Southern white women until the last state, Tennessee, ratified the suffrage amendment.[3] During the debate on ratification there, the *Chattanooga Daily Times* carried an open letter from a Baltimore politician to Tennessee's Governor Roberts. It alleged that woman suffrage would add as many as 70,000 Negro women voters to the electorate of Maryland. "The probabilities are that almost every one of these negro women would actually vote, while it would be extremely difficult to get many of the white women to do so. . . . "[4] White Southern men constantly claimed that black women would vote in large numbers while white "ladies" would remain modestly at home. Thus these men concluded that woman suffrage would bring more blacks than whites to the polls.

Black women voters posed a special threat to Southern political arrangements. Whites prevented black *men* from voting through the use of terrorist tactics, including arson, beating, maiming, castration, and lynching. But "chivalrous" white men sometimes drew the line at employing similar violence against black women. One Mississippi senator told Catt bluntly, "We are not afraid to maul a black man . . . if he dares to vote, but we can't treat women, even black women, that way. No, we'll allow no woman suffrage. It may be right, but we won't have it."[5] W. E. B. DuBois also judged that widespread press attention would prevent Southerners from using violence to keep enfranchised black women from the polls, although he had few illusions about Southern chivalry where black women were concerned. "Even Southern 'gentlemen,' as used as they are to the mistreatment of colored women cannot in the blaze of present publicity physically beat them away from the polls."[6]

---

[3]The first woman suffrage organization in the South seems to have been the South Carolina Woman's Rights Association, an interracial group formed in 1870 with black leadership. See Rosalyn Terborg-Penn, "Afro-Americans in the Struggle for Woman Suffrage" (Ann Arbor MI: University Microfilms, 1977) 55.

[4]Newspaper clipping, Carrie Chapman Catt Papers, Tennessee State Archives, Nashville, Tennessee.

[5]Catt and Shuler, *Woman Suffrage and Politics,* 89. Of course, this statement should not be taken entirely at face value. White supremacists were responsible for horrifying atrocities against black women, even *pregnant* black women.

[6]"Votes for Women," *The Crisis,* November 1917, 8.

At least one powerful Southern politician, Senator Benjamin R. Tillman, believed that black women were more dangerous foes than black men were. He told the editor of a suffrage newspaper, "Experience has taught us that negro women are much more aggressive in asserting the 'rights of that race' than the negro men are."[7] He had no wish to see such implacable opponents of white supremacy gain the added weapon of the ballot.

Finally, white Southern political leaders feared that agitation for woman suffrage in the South would draw unwanted attention to Southern polling practices in general. By the 1890s the federal government had pulled back completely from enforcement of the Fifteenth Amendment guarantee of black male suffrage. Federal officials looked the other way while Southern legislators systematically stripped black men of their right to vote. White Southerners feared that a successful campaign for woman suffrage would reopen the question of suffrage in general. The federal authorities might challenge such Southern state constitutional provisions as the grandfather clause and the poll tax. Southerners feared that discussion of woman suffrage would ultimately open up subjects better left closed.[8]

If white suffragists had spoken out consistently for the civil rights of blacks and/or if they had enforced a policy of racial equality in all NAWSA activities, they would have aroused strong white, Southern antipathy toward woman suffrage. If white suffragists had analyzed how racism as well as sexism barred black women from the polls and if white suffragists had explicitly stated that woman suffrage must include federally enforced access to the polls for black women, they would have played right into the hands of antisuffragists who had a Southern strategy for preventing ratification of woman suffrage. Carrie Chapman Catt informed a colleague,

> The plan of the antis is to find thirteen states which they can hold out against ratification. They have been good enough to give us the list of the states. They are the solid south states. . . . I do not think they would have very much trouble in holding all of these out. Now they will get their thirteenth state in New Jersey, Connecticut, Vermont, or New Hampshire. They tell us so.[9]

If suffragists lost all the Southern states they stood to lose the ratification campaign itself.

-----

[7]Senator B. R. Tillman to Mary Bartlett Dixon, stamped 27 November 1914, NAACP Papers, group I, series C, box 407, Library of Congress, Washington DC.

[8]Aileen S. Kraditor, "Tactical Problems of the Woman-Suffrage Movement in the South," *Louisiana Studies* 5 (Winter 1966): 302-303. See also W. E. B. DuBois, "Votes for Women," *The Crisis*, September 1912, 234.

[9]Catt to Marjorie Shuler, quoted in Flexner, *Century of Struggle*, 330.

Times had changed since the 1860s, when many American reformers supported universal human rights, struggling to advance the cause of women and blacks at the same time. By the last quarter of the nineteenth century the moral fervor that had fueled the antislavery movement and the Civil War was exhausted. The nation sought reconciliation between North and South. If that reconciliation was purchased at the expense of black civil rights, there were few to protest. In the words of Vincent Parrington, "the New England leadership subsided and the tired New England conscience went on vacation."[10]

The tired New England conscience was sorely pressed to deal with immigration and industrialization at home. Carrie Chapman Catt described the late nineteenth century as a period characterized by "inertia in the growth of democracy which has come as a reaction following the aggressive movements that with possibly ill-advised haste enfranchised the foreigner, the negro, and the Indian. Perilous conditions, seeming to follow from the introduction into the body politic of vast numbers of irresponsible citizens, have made the nation timid."[11] Universal suffrage was not a self-evident good. White, native-born suffragists either had to stand for universal suffrage out of season or deemphasize their universal claims, while stressing the numbers of able Anglo-Saxon women whose enfranchisement would benefit society. They chose the latter course.

Universal Rights as a Standard of Accountability

The Failed Vision

White suffragists had a right to concentrate their energies on obtaining political justice for women. They acted on the basis of legitimate group interest when they opposed the Fourteenth and Fifteenth Amendments to the Constitution as hindrances to woman suffrage. Elizabeth Cady Stanton's position was convincing: "If you are a slave, it is your business to break the yoke that galls your own neck; you are to accept slavery and degradation at no price, from no mistaken notions of white men's rights or black men's wrongs."[12] Disturbingly, however, Stanton used hyperbole to describe the plight of white women, who never experienced slavery. She also seemed to deny or to trivialize "black men's wrongs" by connecting them with "mistaken notions."

---

[10]Vincent Louis Parrington, *Main Currents in American Thought,* vol. 3, *The Beginnings of Critical Realism in America: 1860-1920* (New York: Harcourt, Brace and World, 1958) 140.

[11]Ida H. Harper, ed., *The History of Woman Suffrage* (New York: National American Woman Suffrage Association, 1922) 5:6.

[12]Elizabeth Cady Stanton, "Sharp Points," *The Revolution,* 9 April 1868, 212.

In fact, Stanton's Reconstruction-era position was fraught with moral ambiguity. On the one hand, Stanton's ideal policy was the immediate enfranchisement of black men and all women. She genuinely thought that now that the "constitutional door" was open, women should "avail ourselves of the strong arm and blue uniform of the black soldier to walk in by his side, and thus make the gap so wide that no privileged class could ever close it against the humblest citizen of the republic."[13] On the other hand, Stanton was an elitist. She clearly viewed herself and other educated women as superior citizens. Her class elitism combined with racist and nativist prejudice. Stanton stereotyped blacks and immigrants as an ignorant, degraded, and dangerous political element that needed to be outweighed by refined Anglo-Saxon women. In Reconstruction-era debates about suffrage, Stanton used demeaning racial nicknames and appealed to racist and nativist prejudice in her attempt to rouse women and men who shared her race and class privilege to support woman suffrage.

Moreover, Stanton's commitment to *black women's rights* was ambivalent at best. She criticized those reformers who made black male suffrage their highest priority. She accused them of ignoring the needs of one half of the black race. She alleged that her opponents were leaving two million black women "with but a change of masters, still in a condition of slavery."[14] Stanton's own energies were increasingly focused on gaining the ballot for educated, cultured women. Her grudging admission that she would prefer to see Bridget and Dinah enfranchised rather than Patrick and Sambo showed that she did not accept most immigrant and black women as equals.[15] Stanton's appeals to race and class sentiments cannot be condoned.

Nonetheless, white suffragists' assertions of their own political rights were morally permissible. White women were not morally obligated to give strategic priority to black male suffrage after the Civil War. It is difficult to reconstruct fully the political climate of the post-Civil War period.[16]

---

[13]Elizabeth Cady Stanton, Susan B. Anthony, and Mathilda J. Gage, eds., *The History of Woman Suffrage* (New York: Fowler and Wells, 1882) 2:94.

[14]Elizabeth Cady Stanton, "The American Equal Rights Association," *The Revolution*, 27 May 1869, 328.

[15]Elizabeth Cady Stanton, "Equal Rights to All," *The Revolution*, 26 February 1868, 120-21.

[16]While Ellen Carol DuBois is ultimately not critical enough of Stanton's view, she does convey effectively the optimism of some reformers during the earliest days of Reconstruction. This seemed a time of great ferment when profound change was possible. See *Feminism and Suffrage: The Emergence of an Independent Women's Movement in America, 1848-1869* (Ithaca NY: Cornell University Press,

Woman suffrage had a slender chance, if any, to win approval. However, advocating woman suffrage *as an aspect of universal suffrage* was by no means an ignoble position.

Vigorous pursuit of the interest of one's own group in the political arena can be fully legitimate. But a commitment to further the interests of one's own group must be balanced by a willingness to respect the just claims of other members of society as well. Justice requires a moral sensitivity that avoids *both* the Charybdis of perpetual, debilitating sacrifice of group interest and the Scylla of unquestioned, unlimited group assertion.

White women were entitled to demand the vote for themselves, but they should not have used means that degraded black women and men. One technique that white women could have used to hold themselves morally accountable to blacks would have been to measure their own actions against a standard of universal human decency. The American natural rights tradition could have provided such a means to challenge white suffragists' actions that promoted the interests of privileged white women at the unfair expense of other groups.

Appeals to the Anglo-Saxon mystique and the myth of True Womanhood by no means exhausted feminist arguments. As Stanton's 1867 address to the New York state legislature makes clear, suffragists also appealed for justice by invoking the American tradition of political rights. Woman suffragists insisted that a just government derives its authority from the consent of all the governed. Carrie Chapman Catt often spoke about the right of every person to have a voice in government. The principle of citizen consent was forceful *because it was universal,* according to Catt. The consent doctrine served as the foundation, not only for the woman suffrage movement, but also *for other struggles of disadvantaged groups* to seize that political power which was rightfully their own.[17] Stanton agreed that women's problem was to get men to apply long-held, universal principles to women's case.

1978). Eleanor Flexner describes Stanton and her allies as too inexperienced in politics to understand the complex barriers against woman suffrage. She discusses the opposition of the Republican party, which stood to benefit from enfranchising black men, and of many abolitionists, who gave Negro suffrage higher priority. However, Flexner also acknowledges factors that led Stanton and her supporters to believe that universal suffrage might actually be adopted. See *Century of Struggle,* 145-54. Flexner makes an essential qualification when she admits, "from a historical vantage point, their [Stanton and others] optimism seems unfounded" (148). In hindsight, woman suffrage appears to have had almost no chance to be adopted during Reconstruction. But our view of the situation is quite different from the perspective of women immersed in the struggle.

[17]Harper, ed., *History of Woman Suffrage,* 5:21.

There are no new arguments to be made on human rights, our work to-day is to apply to ourselves those so familiar to all; *to teach man that woman is not an anomalous being,* outside all laws and constitutions, *but one whose rights are to be established by the same process of reason as that by which he demands his own.*[18]

Suffragists insisted that the principles of the Declaration of Independence and the Constitution would lose their force if they were denied universality. Speaking for equal rights for blacks and white women, Stanton insisted on the all-embracing character of her principles. "There are no special claims to propose for women and negroes, no new arguments to make in their behalf. . . . As the greater includes the less, an argument for universal suffrage covers the whole question, the rights of all citizens."[19]

In their better moments suffragists demanding full human rights for themselves acknowledged that all fellow human beings—black and white, foreign-born and native-born—were entitled to the same rights. Elizabeth Cady Stanton advised one audience,

[If] "equal rights to all" is the true idea on which to base a government say so, and entrench yourself at that point, hang out the flag of universal suffrage, and do not quarter the enemy on the African to-day, the woman next week, and the Chinaman the week after. Do not involve yourself in the absurdity of demanding an extension of rights by conceding to the Imperialist his principle, admitting that one set of men have the right to limit the natural rights of another.[20]

On such occasions suffragists described America as a nation dedicated to the creation of a society in which all persons are regarded as sharing the same fundamental human worth and in which the basic rights of all human beings are respected. The suffragists did not fault the vision of the just society that their ancestors had bequeathed to them; rather, they chided their contemporaries for disloyalty to that vision.

The moral irony of the American woman suffrage movement is that the suffragists committed the very sin for which they called others to task. They themselves lost sight of the vision of a society in which *all* adults have a voice in government. They insisted on the universality of human rights principles when they were the beneficiaries of a thoroughgoing application of the principles; but, in their concern to defend their own rights, they

---

[18]Stanton, Anthony, and Gage, eds., *History of Woman Suffrage,* 2:349 (emphasis added).

[19]*Proceedings of the First Anniversary of the American Equal Rights Association* (New York: Robert J. Johnston, 1867) 8.

[20]"Butterflies of Fashion," Elizabeth Cady Stanton Papers, box 3, Library of Congress.

gradually turned away from situations in which they were called upon to demand unequivocally those same rights for black women and men.

Universal Human Rights versus Racism

The suffragists' most powerful calls for justice were rooted in a recognition of the equal worth of all human beings as creatures of God. White suffragists abandoned that position when they denigrated the worth of immigrants, Native Americans, and blacks. Carrie Chapman Catt was contemptuous of the Sioux, whom she characterized as murdering, scalping savages. Stanton demeaned blacks and immigrants, using degrading nicknames such as Sambo, Patrick, and Yung Tung. She joined Carrie Chapman Catt in asserting that the vast number of new immigrants were drawn from the worst elements in Europe. These immigrants were pictured as a threat to America's democratic institutions, not as fellow creatures of God entitled to the same rights accorded to the native-born. Stanton reprimanded congressmen for the injustice done to the Saxon woman "by exalting another race above her head: slaves, ignorant, degraded, depraved, but yesterday crouching at your feet."[21] Ironically, a former abolitionist—Stanton—now saw yesterday's slaves as a dangerous element, not properly entitled to political rights unless those rights were also accorded to Anglo-Saxon women. By contrasting immigrant and black men who were "illiterate and degraded" with Anglo-Saxon women who were "educated and refined," white suffragists undermined the force of their claim that all persons were entitled to share political power. The right of all adults to vote is based not on the contribution they make to the social welfare by the expression of their wise opinions, but rather on their individual right to participate in the process by which community life is shaped.

White suffragists retreated from an acknowledgment of the dignity of all human beings when they began to argue that some persons (upper-class Anglo-Saxon women) were more qualified to vote than were some others (lower-class blacks and immigrants). If all the people constitute the government by offering their voluntary consent at the ballot box, then no citizen (who is capable of voting) is more or less qualified than any other, for all citizens share the one and only relevant qualification—an adult human nature.

Anna Howard Shaw recognized the moral loss white suffragists inflicted upon the movement when they made overtly racist appeals. In private correspondence Shaw argued that the NAWSA should repudiate claims that woman suffrage would safeguard white supremacy throughout the South lest it appear that "we really don't believe in the justice of

---

[21]"Mrs. Stanton Before the District Committee," *The Revolution*, 4 February 1869, 88.

suffrage, but simply that certain classes or races should dominate the government." Shaw also argued for the primacy of universal human rights as a moral position in her first address as president of the NAWSA. Shaw reminded her audience that any social movement must have both an ideal and an organization to promote that ideal. However, as a social movement begins to experience some success, there is a temptation to compromise the ideal in order to build a more effective social organization. Shaw understood the seductive lure of policies that would enhance the numerical strength and/or public influence of a social movement at the expense of a clear advocacy of its original principles. So she cautioned that the suffrage movement must not grow silent concerning its own highest principles, but ever more clearly articulate them in its public discourse.

> We must guard against the reactionary spirit which marks our time, and stand unfalteringly for the principle of perfect equality of rights and opportunities for all. *We must refuse to restrict our demand for justice or bound it by any line or race, sex, creed, or any other condition which does not apply equally to every citizen of the republic.*[22]

Black suffragist Anna Julia Cooper also urged suffragists to be loyal to the movement's broadest vision. She judged that the women's movement was of great moral significance because it was "an embodiment, if its pioneers could only realize it, of the universal good." Cooper was convinced that when race, color, sex, and condition no longer nullified a person's inalienable right to life, liberty, and the pursuit of happiness, "then woman's lesson is taught and woman's cause is won—not the white woman nor the black woman nor the red woman, but the cause of every man or woman who has writhed silently under a mighty wrong." Cooper believed that white women's rights were inextricably linked to the rights of all other human beings. Any tactic that obscured that link diminished the moral force of the woman suffrage movement.[23]

Cooper understood the pressure white Southerners were exerting on the women's movement. She appreciated the firm commitment to principle that was required to refrain from advancing only the narrow interests of privileged white women. It was very tempting to promote the rights of such women at the expense of blacks, immigrants, and Native Americans. "But, may it not be that, as women, the very lessons which seem

---

[22]Shaw to Laura Clay, 15 November 1906, Laura Clay Papers, Special Collections, University of Kentucky, Lexington KY; Wilmer A. Linkugel, "The Speeches of Anna Howard Shaw: Collected and Edited with Introduction and Notes," 2 vols. (Ph.D. diss., University of Wisconsin, 1961) 2:471 (emphasis added).

[23]Anna J. Cooper, *A Voice from the South* (Xenia OH: Aldine Printing House, 1892) 121, 125.

hardest to master now, are possibly the ones most essential for our promotion to a higher grade of work?"[24]

Unfortuately, Shaw and Cooper were never able to persuade their fellow suffragists that compromising their call for universal human rights would be fatal to the moral significance of the suffrage movement. So women won the vote, but lost the soul of a movement that originally had advocated full political rights for all citizens of the republic—female as well as male, black as well as white, foreign-born as well as native-born.

Racism and True Womanhood

White suffragists' racist arguments and actions clearly contradicted their demand for a recognition of universal political rights. In addition, their appeals to the myth of True Womanhood were often tainted by class bias and hence also by implicit racial and ethnic prejudice. The argument that women as life bearers have a greater respect for life and would demand legislation protective of life is a statement potentially true of women from every race, ethnic group, and class. But the idealization of women as homemakers and full-time child-rearers reflected a limited middle- and upper-class experience. The full-time mother and housewife was more likely to be white and native-born. Poor women disproportionately drawn from the black, Native American, or immigrant groups were often unable to maintain a home that could serve as a model for municipal order and cleanliness. Aileen Kraditor reminds us that immigrant women "rarely lived in big houses on tree-lined streets, but rather . . . [in] overcrowded tenements in which the mother could hardly be a queen or the home a realm."[25] Such was also the situation of poor native-born women of every race.

The education, the refinement, and the moral purity that the True Woman would bring to the polls were also largely the prerogative of upper-class women. Gerda Lerner has demonstrated that, at the very time the True Woman was most extolled, many poor mill women were being exploited by an explosive industrialization that put education and refinement beyond their reach. Moreover, that "moral purity" typified by orthodox sexual behavior was an unaffordable luxury for too many poor women. Compliance with the sexual demands of foremen and employers was far too often necessary in order to keep a job. In other cases, prostitution was the economic alternative to the sweatshop.[26]

---

[24]Ibid., 84.

[25]Aileen Kraditor, *Ideas of the Woman Suffrage Movement: 1890-1920* (New York: Anchor Books, 1971) 105.

[26]See Gerda Lerner, "The Lady and the Mill Girl: Changes in the Status of

In addition, white male mythology differentiated sharply between the legendary purity of the white wife and mother and the imagined availability, if not promiscuity, of the black woman.[27] All too often white males sexually harassed and assaulted black women. Thus, when suffragists spoke of the True Woman, their portrait usually fit only white, upper-class women, not half of the entire human race fully entitled to their human rights.

Sojourner Truth's famous "Ain't I a Woman" speech illuminates the class and racial biases that were a frequent backdrop for white suffragists' talk about True Womanhood. Truth was an ex-slave who was an advocate for black and women's rights. In 1851 she attended a women's rights meeting in Akron, Ohio, where male members of the audience initially dominated the meeting with arguments against women's rights. Male speakers had insisted that women were too delicate to participate in public life. Finally, Truth rose and approached the podium. Racist supporters of woman suffrage hissed warnings that she not be allowed to speak. Nevertheless, the white woman presiding allowed her to address the group. Truth's powerful speech swayed the assembly in favor of women's rights. She rebutted the accusation that women were too weak to handle political rights. Truth pointed out that she did not receive chivalrous attentions. No one helped her over puddles or into carriages. "And ain't I a woman?" Displaying her powerful arm muscles, she insisted that she could plow or plant or harvest as much as any man. "And ain't I a woman?" Society gave her—a black woman—no special privileges because of her sex. Indeed, her suffering was heavier because she was a woman. "I have borne thirteen children and seen them most all sold off to slavery, and when I cried out with my mother's grief, none but Jesus heard me."[28] Even as that highest representative of True Womanhood—a mother—society had given this former slave no special honor or prerogatives.

Black women like Sojourner Truth were in a position to make clear that womanliness actually had nothing to do with the trappings of class privilege. As the editor of *Woman's Era* proclaimed, "womanliness . . . is

---

Women in the Age of Jackson," *Midcontinent American Studies Journal* 10 (Spring 1969): 5-15; and Mary Bulzarik, "Sexual Harassment at the Workplace: Historical Notes," *Radical America* 12 (July/August 1978): 25-43. For material on this dilemma as it existed in a comparable society, Victorian England, see E. M. Sigsworth and T. J. Wyke, "A Study of Victorian Prostitution and Venereal Disease," in *Suffer and Be Still,* ed. Martha Vicinus (Bloomington: Indiana University Press, 1973) 77-99.

[27]Calvin Hernton, *Sex and Racism in America* (New York: Grove Press, 1965) 123-28.

[28]Elizabeth Cady Stanton, Susan B. Anthony, and Mathilda J. Gage, eds., *The History of Woman Suffrage* (New York: Fowler and Wells, 1881) 1:115-17.

not supplied or withdrawn by surroundings, it may be lacking in the most feeble and protected woman, and strong in her who is the support of her little ones and has to fight the flesh, the devil and the world too, in their behalf."[29]

The Price of Integrity

If the suffragists had continued to state clearly that they favored the vote for women as an aspect of the universal human right to a voice in government, the passage of the Nineteenth Amendment could have been seriously delayed. If they had frankly acknowledged that the logic of their position encompassed genuine access to the polls for blacks and immigrants, the chance to get the vote in 1920 would have been jeopardized. The fate of the contemporary Equal Rights Amendment shows that, if Southern states remain solidly opposed to an amendment benefiting women, passage is almost impossible, since unanimous approval by all Northern and Western states is extremely unlikely. With some Southern support, the woman suffrage amendment was ratified in fourteen months; without Southern backing, the ERA was not ratified in ten years.[30]

Once it became clear that a federal constitutional amendment would be necessary in order to ensure woman suffrage, suffragists needed the support of at least some white Southern politicians. However, most white Southerners opposed any public policy that threatened white supremacy. Woman suffragists faced a hard choice: they could pander to white supremacists in order to gain the ballot, or they could stand for woman suffrage as one aspect of universal suffrage—white and black, male and female—and lose crucial political support.

White suffragists were entitled to press for woman suffrage as a priority, but they were wrong to use racist means to obtain their goal. They eviscerated the moral power of the woman suffrage movement when they denigrated black, Native American, and immigrant men and when they manipulated the myth of True Womanhood without insisting that genuine womanliness was not dependent on race and class privilege. White suffragists should have refrained from using racist and nativist argu-

---

[29]"Woman's Place," *Woman's Era*, September 1894, 8.

[30]There are limits to this comparison. First, the Nineteenth Amendment offered women one clearly defined benefit—the right to vote—which, by 1920, did not radically affect existing social arrangements. The ERA prohibits all discrimination under law on the basis of sex. It is not entirely clear how courts would interpret this amendment, but social changes wrought as a result of the amendment could be far reaching. Thus, the ERA is more threatening to social conservatives. Second, the Nineteenth Amendment was the chief priority of a major woman's movement under the leadership of an organizational genius, Carrie Chapman Catt. The ERA is only one of the goals of the more fragmented latter-day movement which, as yet, lacks such leadership.

ments even at the cost of delaying passage of a woman suffrage amendment. When these white suffragists squandered the moral capital of the natural rights tradition in order to ensure prompt ratification of the Nineteenth Amendment, they impoverished their moral legacy for twentieth-century women and men.[31]

Woman Suffrage and Contemporary Feminism

The history of racism within the woman suffrage movement has important implications for the contemporary feminist movement. The woman suffrage movement had a bold vision and noble principles. In its best moments it was a movement dedicated to the rights of black women, immigrant women, Native American women, working-class women, poor women—all women, not just economically privileged white women.

But this is also a story of a vision betrayed. For the white women who led this movement came to trade upon their privilege as the daughters (sisters, wives, and mothers) of powerful white men in order to gain for themselves some share of the political power those men possessed. They did not adequately identify ways in which that political power would not be equally accessible to poor women, immigrant women, and black women. As a group, white woman suffrage leaders did not develop strategies to ensure that the access to the ballot box guaranteed in principle by the Nineteenth Amendment would become a reality for most black women.

In theological terms, a study of racism in the woman suffrage movement is a study of the enduring reality of human sinfulness. Human sin has been an important topic in feminist theology. Contemporary feminist theologians have challenged the inappropriate identification of women with evil. We have named patriarchy as sin and have offered detailed descriptions of its multiple manifestations. We have probed women's complicity with our own oppressors. All of these lines of investigation are

---

[31]Historian William L. O'Neill also castigates woman suffrage leaders for squandering the moral capital of the suffrage movement. However, he believes that they sold out their integrity for a franchise that was of little real value. He views the vote as of little worth to women because, at the time when he was writing, women had not used their franchise to foster a single important political or social change for women. See *Everyone Was Brave: A History of Feminism in America* (New York: Quadrangle/The New York Times Book Co., 1971). While O'Neill admits that a demand for the fair application of democratic principles was the suffragists' strongest argument, he underplays the importance of woman suffrage as a human rights issue. The success of the woman suffrage movement was a vindication of women's right to vote, whether or not women use that political power to advance their interests as women. In my opinion, O'Neill also underestimates the real, albeit limited, power to influence legislation that women gained. Women have had the vote so long that most people have forgotten how difficult it was for women to influence public policy without the vote.

important and need to be pursued. However, feminist theologians have given less attention to other aspects of women's experience of sin. A careful analysis of racism in the woman suffrage movement provides an instructive case study of feminist sinfulness.

A review of the history of the woman suffrage movement demonstrates the importance of understanding sin as *both* individual wrongs and as perversions in social structures. Stanton had morally offensive attitudes toward persons of lesser education and "refinement" and she coupled those views with demeaning racial and ethnic stereotypes. Catt seems to have had strong fearful and negative attitudes toward Native Americans. Nonetheless, Stanton, Shaw, and Catt were also women of integrity who had a genuine commitment to the struggle for the recognition of the rights of all women. In my judgment, these women did not passively condone Southern segregation practices and actively manipulate racist ideology solely, or even primarily, because of personal bad intentions. These white woman suffrage leaders made their strategic choices to use racist ideology to their own advantage within the context of a racist society that put intense political pressure upon them. In a racist society these women had severely limited choices. They did, however, have the option of actively resisting racism, although at the likely cost of a significant delay in obtaining woman suffrage.

Sin is not the only, or the final, theological word in response to the history of the woman suffrage movement. It is important also to speak about grace—the empowering of persons to change their orientation toward racism, to make a firm commitment to the struggle for racial justice, to develop new relationships characterized by mutual respect between black and white people, and to join in transforming social structures so that social institutions will sustain, not impede, mutuality. Grace empowers white women to examine critically the impact of our attitudes and actions on black persons; grace enriches white women with the wisdom to balance assertions of our own claims for justice with a commitment to do justice to others who suffer forms of oppression we do not share; grace strengthens white women to remain faithful to the long process of transforming sexist, racist, and classist structures. Grace is the basis for what Anna Julia Cooper called a "courageous, unwavering, stalwart heart."[32]

The history of the woman suffrage movement also highlights the limitations of the myth of True Womanhood. An investigation of the limitations of this myth is important, because it is being revived in new ways by some contemporary feminists. Some feminists are asserting once again that women *as women* have a special moral sensitivity—one not shared by men. This new version of the myth of True Womanhood could be dangerous to the extent that it obscures feminists' capacity for sin. To the ex-

---

[32]Cooper, *Voice from the South,* 100.

tent that some white feminists come to believe that they are part of a female moral elite, they may be less self-critical on issues such as race.[33]

In order for those who are white feminists to be self-critical of our racism, we must be part of communities in which we are held responsible for the impact of our actions on the black community. The severing of ties between the black freedom movement and the women's movement during the Reconstruction period left too many nineteenth-century white feminists without structures of accountability on racial issues. After the American Equal Rights Association collapsed, leaders of the National Woman Suffrage Association and its successor (NAWSA) were no longer a part of larger structures in which black women and men could critique their actions as peers.[34] Black feminists and some white feminists did challenge racism in the woman suffrage movement, but their criticism does not seem to have elicited a sustained and serious response.

In the absence of structures to sustain mutual accountability among white and black feminists, white feminist leaders all too often ignored black women's distinctive experiences and priorities. Incidents such as the defeat of the resolution calling for adequate railroad car accommodations for black women seem to demonstrate that many white feminists were ignorant of or unconcerned about the special burdens of black feminists who were subject to both racism and sexism. White, middle- and upper-class feminists appear to have held a largely unexamined assumption that what benefited them would automatically benefit other less socially privileged women. The Nineteenth Amendment to the Constitution passed, but it did little to ensure a voice in government for large numbers of black women. In the late twentieth century, there is still a strong risk that many

---

[33] Whether there are new black feminist versions of the myth of True Womanhood is an interesting question that deserves further investigation.

[34] I disagree with the interpretation of Ellen Carol DuBois who sees the breakup of the American Equal Rights Association in a positive light. She views the association between the women's rights movement and the abolitionist movement as an eventual dead end for white feminists. She acknowledges that the association between the two causes originally provided women with an egalitarian ideology, a theory of social change, a network of contacts and resources, and an opportunity to gain leadership skills and self-confidence. Eventually, however, the women's movement found itself trapped in a debilitating dependency on male abolitionists for resources, ideology, and strategies. She suggests that, when Stanton and her allies created the NWSA, they were taking necessary steps toward creating an autonomous women's movement that could challenge women to analyze their own oppression and to mobilize as women to demand sexual equality. DuBois does not, however, analyze the role of black women in this new woman suffrage movement which focused on sexual oppression. Nor does she acknowledge that the racist attitudes and actions of white suffragists lost needed restraints. See DuBois, *Feminism and Suffrage*.

white feminists will remain ignorant about the experiences and priorities of black feminists and that white feminists will devise strategies too limited to contribute to the liberation of all women.

5 | Black Women's Perspectives on Feminism

CONTEMPORARY WHITE FEMINISTS do not appeal explicitly to an ideology of white supremacy. Most repudiate the Anglo-Saxon mystique and vigorously affirm the equal human dignity of all persons. Yet those of us who are white feminists are still prone to exhibit racism by ignoring the experiences of black people. Too often we describe our own experiences as if they represented universal human experience, thus acting as if black women simply did not exist. Moreover, we have a tendency to propose social changes meant to benefit all women without analyzing how racist social structures may distort the impact of those proposals.

If the contemporary feminist movement is to gain the power to liberate all women, then its theory and practice must incorporate the concerns and experiences of black women. An increasing number of black feminists are speaking out about the experiences and goals of black women. Their writings reveal that black women frequently have a distinctive perspective on feminist issues. Those of us who are white feminists have a responsibility to inform ourselves about the issues black women raise and to support black women in their self-defined struggle for liberation.

Black feminists have something special to say about issues such as rape, work, male/female solidarity, and female beauty.[1] Black women are, of course, individuals and, as such, each has her own unique perspective. I

---

[1] I have selected these four issues because they seem to be important issues for black writers and also because they help me to understand the particularity of my experience as a middle-class white woman. I do not want to suggest that I as a white woman set the standards for "authentic" black experience. Most especially I do not want to suggest that black women who disagree with what they read below are not really "black" or not genuine "black feminists." It is for black women to define what black feminism means. Bell Hooks makes a powerful criticism of those white feminists who set up one narrow stereotype of authentic black experience. She also denounces paternalistic white women who set themselves up as experts on racism capable of mediating black women's experience to racist white women. See *Feminist Theory from Margin to Center* (Boston: South End Press, 1984) 11-12. Some black women committed to the liberation of women prefer to create their own words to name their commitment. Alice Walker has suggested the word "womanist." See *In Search of Our Mothers' Gardens: Womanist Prose* (San Diego: Harcourt Brace Jovanovich, 1983) xi-xii.

have combined materials from the writings of many black women to describe some themes that seem to me to be emphasized when black women write about feminism. Individual black women would certainly differ with some of the views presented here. Moreover, these four issues by no means exhaust the subjects on which black women have voiced special concerns.

I have criticized white leaders of the woman suffrage movement for failure to acknowledge the distinctive experiences of black women and for failure to respond creatively to criticisms of racism within the movement. One technique that can help to minimize such failures today is active listening. Those of us who are white feminists need to take the initiative to inform ourselves about the distinctive experiences, theories, and strategies of black feminists. We need to invite black women into dialogue through the act of "hearing them into speech."[2] Part of this process of active listening includes discussing the statements of black women in order to acknowledge the importance of what they are saying and to create an opportunity for them to correct any misunderstandings.

Rape

The women's liberation movement has spawned a vigorous antirape movement determined to end sexual violence against women. The antirape movement has adopted a wide variety of tactics. Women have educated people about the realities of rape, challenging such myths as "no woman can be raped unless she wants to be"; "a rapist is a sexually frustrated male who acts on impulse to gratify his lust"; and "if you were raped, you must have invited it." Feminists have learned self-defense techniques, demanded humane treatment from police officers and health workers who deal with rape victims, and proposed legal reforms designed to protect the rape victim in court and to increase the number of convictions for rape.

Obtaining rape convictions has been particularly difficult. "In reported rape cases where the police *do* believe the victim, only 51 percent of the offenders are actually apprehended, and of these, 76 percent are prosecuted, and of these, 47 percent are acquitted or have their cases dismissed."[3] Thus, less than 21 percent of the *reported* rape cases result in conviction of the rapist. A 1978 federal study showed that only one in five rapes is reported, only one of four reported rapes results in an arrest, and only one in 60 arrests ends in conviction.[4] Several cities, including New York, have established special prosecution units within district attorneys'

[2]This phrase was suggested to me by Nelle Morton, "The Rising Woman Consciousness in a Male Language Structure," *Andover Newton Quarterly* 12 (March 1972): 177-90.

[3]Susan Brownmiller, *Against Our Will: Men, Women, and Rape* (New York: Bantam Books, 1975) 190.

[4]*New York Times,* 7 August 1978, A8.

offices to handle rape cases. These units have a much better conviction record. Nevertheless, many rapes are unreported, and many rapists are never arrested or convicted. Susan Brownmiller demonstrates how police officers compound the problem when they unfairly declare that some rape reports are unfounded, especially if the complainant is a minority woman. Some white police officers stereotype minority women as promiscuous, then assume that a promiscuous woman cannot be raped. (After all, if you don't save yourself for one man, you are automatically fair game for any man.)

Black women decry the myth of the sexually available black woman. They are outraged that this myth continues to be used to excuse sexual violence against black women. White Americans have historically stereotyped black people as people possessed of bestial sexual passions. Many white Americans fantasize that the black female is capable of free, passionate sexual encounters that are impossible for the frigid white "lady." Black women have come to expect a special form of sexual harassment from white men aroused by white fantasies about black women. Black women, from young teenagers to women in late middle age, are sexually harassed on the streets by a stream of white men who assume that every black woman is a "hot number" and likely a prostitute. In the 1960s black playwright Lorraine Hansberry had one of her characters lament,

> I can be coming home from eight hours on an assembly line or fourteen hours in Mrs. Halsey's kitchen. I can be all filled up that day with three hundred years of rage so that my eyes are flashing and my flesh is trembling—and the white boys in the streets, they look at me and think of sex. They look at me and that's all they think.[5]

The myth of the passionate, promiscuous black woman created the social stimulus and permission for a form of interracial rape cloaked in social secrecy and denial—the rape of black women by white men. Bell Hooks demonstrates the depth of white denial of white on black rape in her critique of the chapter "A Question of Race" in Susan Brownmiller's book on rape.[6] When discussing "interracial rape," Brownmiller emphasizes the rape of white women by black men. When Brownmiller does discuss white rape of black women, she treats it primarily as a historic issue, focusing on the rape of black slave women, but providing much less information about interracial rape of black women after Emancipation. Black women state candidly that they continue to be the victims of racist sexual violence.

---

[5]Lorraine Hansberry, quoted in Bell Hooks, *Ain't I a Woman: Black Women and Feminism* (Boston: South End Press, 1981) 58.

[6]Hooks, *Ain't I a Woman*, 51-52.

Rape statistics must be interpreted with caution, since many rape survivors refuse to make official police reports of the crime. Still, there is some evidence that black women are the targets of rapists more frequently than white women.[7] Therefore, it might seem that antirape campaigns could unite black and white women. But that it is not always the case.

Some black women see antirape measures as a racist threat to black men. While white police officers have too often labeled as unfounded black women's rape reports, they are diligent in their pursuit of black men charged with the rape of white women. Once arrested, a black man is far more likely to be convicted and far more likely to receive a tough sentence. According to statistics cited by Angela Davis, "of the 455 men executed between 1930 and 1967 for rape convictions, 405 of them were black."[8] When the charge is interracial rape, black women fear that a racist judicial system will mete out severe sentences to black men, while treating white men more leniently.

Black women are also concerned that innocent black men will be found guilty of rape. They cannot forget the number of black men who were lynched on trumped-up rape charges. The archetypal figure in this context is Emmett Till, the fourteen-year-old boy who was beaten and killed, his body mutilated and thrown in the river, because he had whistled at a white woman and then bragged to her husband that he had "had" white women before. In her poem "Afterimages" the poet Audre Lorde invokes the bond that many black women feel with Till. She recalls how his murder was emblazoned across New York newsstands in 1955: "he was baptized my son forever in the midnight waters of the Pearl."[9] Black women feel a deep kinship with those black men who have been offered as sacrificial victims on the idolatrous altar of "pure white womanhood."

Several black women have responded angrily to Susan Brownmiller's treatment of the Till case in *Against Our Will.* Brownmiller, while condemning Emmett Till's murder and the mutilation of his body, criticizes Till for sexual harassment of Carolyn Bryant. Brownmiller interprets Till's whistle, hurled back at Bryant after she had ordered him out of her store with a gun, as an assertion of male dominance. "Emmett Till was going to show his black buddies that he, and by inference *they,* could get a white woman and Carolyn Bryant was the nearest convenient object. In con-

---

[7]Mary Pellauer, "Moral Callousness and Moral Sensitivity: Violence Against Women," in *Women's Consciousness, Women's Conscience,* ed. Barbara Hilkert Andolsen, Christine E. Gudorf, and Mary D. Pellauer (Minneapolis: Winston/Seabury Press, 1985) 38.

[8]Angela Davis, "Rape, Racism and the Capitalist Setting," *The Black Scholar* 9 (April 1978): 24.

[9]Audre Lorde, "Afterimages," *Chosen Poems—Old and New* (New York: W. W. Norton and Company, 1982) 103.

crete terms, the accessibility of *all* white women was on review." Brownmiller concludes that, in that situation (with Till running out of the store chased at gunpoint), his whistle was "a deliberate insult just short of physical assault, a last reminder to Carolyn Bryant that this black boy, Till, had in mind to possess her." Angela Davis castigates Brownmiller for blaming the victim, grossly exaggerating the significance of Till's gesture. Davis accuses Brownmiller of painting a portrait of Till "as a guilty sexist—almost as guilty as his white racist murderers." According to Davis, the work of several white feminists who have written about rape has helped to resuscitate the myth of the wild-eyed black male rapist.[10]

Black leaders and woman suffragists Mary Church Terrell, Ida B. Wells-Barnett, and Frederick Douglass insisted that the stereotype of the sexually insatiable black rapist arose after Reconstruction as whites sought forcibly to reinstitute white supremacy throughout the South.[11] Frederick Douglass pointed out that there was never any accusation of wholesale rape of Southern white women by black male slaves during the Civil War in spite of the absence of white women's white male "protectors." During the first years of Reconstruction, white Southerners initially justified the murders of scores of black women and men as a means to prevent widespread antiwhite insurrections. Next, whites candidly admitted that antiblack violence was a means to reinstate white supremacy. When the number of lynchings increased while white dominance was firmly reestablished, white Southerners needed a new way to legitimate their violence, so they alleged that the black men they lynched had raped white women and girls. Ignoring the fact that black women were among those lynched, they claimed that lynching was necessary to stem a rising tide of sexual violence.

Lynching was used as a weapon against black men who were alleged to be rapists, but whose real crime was business success or political leadership. Acceptance of the myth of the black rapist by white Americans made lynching seem justifiable as a distasteful but necessary means to protect white womanhood. Black people bitterly resented both the silence about the sexual violence that black women experienced and the ways a

---

[10]Brownmiller, *Against Our Will*, 272-73; Angela Davis, *Women, Race, and Class* (New York: Random House, 1981) 178-82.

[11]Mary Church Terrell, "Lynching from a Negro's Point of View," Mary Church Terrell Papers, reel 21, Library of Congress, Washington DC; Ida B. Wells-Barnett, excerpt from "U.S. Atrocities," in *Black Women in Nineteenth-Century American Life*, ed. Bert James Loewenberg and Ruth Bogin (University Park PA: Pennsylvania State University Press, 1976) 253-62; Frederick Douglass, "Why is the Negro Lynched?" in *The Life and Writings of Frederick Douglass*, ed. Philip S. Foner (New York: International Publishers, 1955) 4:491-523.

warped protectiveness (that was really possessiveness and white male control) of white womanhood was used to excuse violence against blacks.

Twisted sexual tensions poisoned relationships between the races. Frederick Douglass declared that the "perpetual reiterations in our newspapers and magazines" of the stereotype of the black male rapist led white women and men to regard the black man "with averted eyes, dark suspicion and increasing hate."[12] As a result of this history, black women are wary of white feminist campaigns against rape.

Rape charges continue to be a pretext for deadly violence against black men. In Milwaukee in 1981, a black youth was arrested by white policemen as a suspect in a rape. He died of injuries received in the arrest. The young man, Ernest Lacy, did not fit the description of the rapist. Shortly after his arrest and death, the rape victim identified another man as her assailant. Lacy, who had a history of mental illness, apparently ran from police when they attempted to question him in connection with the rape that had occurred minutes before. According to the white police officers, Lacy struggled with them. Witnesses allege that the police then wrestled Lacy to the ground. One white officer put his knee between Lacy's shoulder blades and lifted Lacy's arms above his head. Medical experts consulted by the Lacy family believe that this maneuver cut off oxygen to Lacy's brain and was the direct cause of his death. A coroner's inquest recommended charges of homicide as a result of reckless conduct, but the charges were subsequently dropped.[13]

This case came to my attention when Ernest Lacy's mother appeared on a black radio station in New York City. Callers flooded the station with expressions of sympathy. Many black mothers called to say that they feared that their sons could be victims of the same kind of violence. More than one caller mentioned Emmett Till. Black women, especially black mothers, experience fears for young black men that white women do not experience. Black poet Audre Lorde names this reality when she says to white women, "You fear your children will grow up to join the patriarchy and testify against you, we fear our children will be dragged from a car and shot down in the street, and you will turn your backs upon the reasons they are dying."[14]

A 1977 rape case in Madison, Wisconsin, illustrates how rape charges can polarize white and black women. In this incident, three black youths were found guilty of raping a white girl in the stairwell of a high school. The judge allowed the youngest defendant (a fifteen-year-old) to return

[12]Douglass, "Why is the Negro Lynched?" 503.

[13]*New York Times*, 16 August 1981, 26.

[14]Audre Lorde, "Age, Race, Class and Sex: Women Redefining Difference," in *Sister Outsider: Essays and Speeches* (Trumansburg NY: Crossing Press, 1984) 119.

home under court supervision. The case drew national attention when the judge justified the light sentence he had given the fifteen-year-old by describing rape as a "normal" adolescent reaction to the provocative dress of contemporary women. Feminist pressure, focusing on the issue of sexism, led to the recall of the judge. Madison's white feminists were enraged because the judge's remarks trivialized rape and transferred blame to the victim, the allegedly provocative girl. Madison's black leaders refused to accept a definition of the situation that excluded racism as an element. White outrage at the light sentence given to one black defendant had resulted in a white judge's recall. Blacks feared that other judges watching the election would draw the conclusion that their chances of continuing in office would be improved if they meted out harsh sentences to black criminals. Finally, blacks pointed to the judge's reputation for fairness in cases involving blacks; they alleged that elements in the white community were using his rape remarks as a convenient excuse to get rid of an otherwise liberal judge. Tension between Madison's white and black women was reflected in remarks by local black rights leader Eloise Anderson-Addison. "My problem with the women's movement is that white women can't deal with their own racism. This is a classical example of that conflict."[15]

Those of us who are white feminists must work with black feminists to devise strategies that protect all women from sexual violence. We need to address racism directly when analyzing the inadequacies of the judicial system in restraining and deterring sexual violence. Given the history of white violence against black men accused of interracial rape, we must make it clear that we condemn the use of excessive force in the apprehension of black suspects. White feminists should be disturbed by the disparity among the penalties meted out to men guilty of comparable assaults. We should lend support to efforts to ensure that white and black men guilty of similar crimes receive similar sentences.

Work

The issue of work, particularly paid domestic work, has divided white and black feminists. In the late 1960s and early 1970s, middle- and upperclass predominately white feminists emphasized the financial independence and personal fulfillment women could achieve if they were allowed equal access to paid employment.

After World War II middle-class white women were left isolated in suburban homes. Most black women and an increasing number of white women were already in the paid work force. It was middle-class white housewives who, therefore, tended to idealize the work place as the arena of freedom. Middle-class white feminists tended to emphasize managerial and especially professional jobs as their model of employment. They pic-

---

[15]*New York Times*, 15 June 1977, A17.

tured women in jobs such as doctor, bank executive, teacher, or social worker. These jobs provide opportunities for work that is varied, demands personal initiative, and pays relatively well.

While a number of middle-class white women were trapped in their suburban homes, most black women were continuing a long established ethnic pattern—working for their family's survival in the economic world. After Emancipation, most black women worked as farm laborers or domestic workers and laundresses. A few worked in menial factory jobs. Those black women with a better education were concentrated in the teaching field. In the late 1960s a small but growing number of black women were employed as clerical and service workers. Black women worked, but few black women experienced work as a source of fulfillment or real financial independence.

Thus, middle-class white and working-class black women have significantly different experiences of work, but their experiences intersect in the roles of black domestic and white employer. It is especially important to look at domestic work because it was one of the major forms of work available to black women from the end of slavery until the civil rights movement of the 1960s. It is only in the past two decades, since equal employment laws have been federally enforced, that large numbers of younger black women have been able to get other service and clerical jobs. Young black women who have other employment opportunities are choosing not to do domestic work.

Black women working as domestics have suffered terrible exploitation. Domestic workers worked long hours at low pay. When the relationship between white mistress and black domestic was at its worst, the black woman was little better than a slave. Witness the anonymous account given by one domestic in 1912.

> I frequently work from fourteen to sixteen hours a day. I am compelled . . . to sleep in the house. I am allowed to go home to my children, the oldest of whom is a girl of 18 years, only once in two weeks, every other Sunday afternoon—even then I am not permitted to stay all night. I not only have to nurse a little white child, now eleven months old, but I have to act as playmate . . . to three other children in the home, the oldest of whom is only nine years of age. I wash and dress the baby two or three times a day; I give it its meals, mainly from a bottle; I have to put it to bed each night; and, in addition, I have to get up and attend to its every call between midnight and morning. If the baby falls asleep during the day, as it has been trained to do every day about eleven o'clock, I am not permitted to rest. It's "Mammy, do this," or "Mammy, do that," or "Mammy, do the other," from my mistress all the time. . . . I see my children only when they happen to see me on the streets when I am out with the children, or when my children come to the

"yard" to see me, which isn't often, because my white folks don't like to see their servants' children hanging around the premises. You might as well say that I'm on duty all the time—from sunrise to sunrise, every day of the week. I am the slave, body and soul, of this family.[16]

As this poignant reading makes clear, working-class black women often were unavailable to mother their own children, because they were working in white homes to earn enough money to provide for the physical survival of those black children. Such black women were paid to nurture white children, while they worked under conditions that limited the time and energy they could devote to their own young ones.

Black domestics suffered because they received low wages and often no fringe benefits. Employers who demanded live-in arrangements were sometimes particularly exploitative. Their domestics often worked even longer hours, got little disposable income, and were separated from their families and their own communities. Black women who were day workers had particularly unreliable incomes. An employer might suddenly declare that the day worker's services were not needed for a period of time (such as the employers' vacation) and leave the worker with no pay for the days left open.

A frequent grievance of black household workers was that they were cheated out of full payment of already low wages. White employers were particularly notorious for giving their employees used clothing in place of cash. While the growing scarcity of domestic workers has alleviated some problems, the wage of domestic workers remains low. In 1983, according to Department of Labor statistics, the average *weekly* earnings for a "private household cleaner or servant" was one hundred thirty-five dollars.[17] And workers are often without health insurance or adequate retirement provisions.

Animosity continues between white and black women over the exploitation of black women as domestics. The famed civil rights leader, Fannie Lou Hamer, reported feeling anger when she found her white employer claiming credit for Hamer's labor.

You know, I remember a time when I was working around white people's house, and one thing that would make me mad as hell, after I would be done slaved all day long, this white woman would get on the phone . . . and said, "You know, I'm tired because *we* have been working," and I said, "That's a damn lie." You are not used

---

[16]"I Live a Treadmill Life," in *Black Women in White America: A Documentary History,* ed. Gerda Lerner (New York: Vintage Books, 1972) 227-28.

[17]Earl F. Mellor, "Weekly Earnings in 1983," *Monthly Labor Review* 108 (January 1985): 57.

to that kind of language, honey, but I'm gone to tell you where it's *at*. So all these things was happening because you [the white woman] *had* more. You had been put on a pedestal, and then not only put on a pedestal, but you had been put in something like an ivory castle.[18]

There is a complex relationship between the economically privileged white woman trapped in a gilded cage and the poor black woman employed to polish that cage. "The black woman was needed and valued by the white female as a domestic. The black female diluted much of the oppression of the white female by the white male."[19] Black women who have been exploited to provide time for economically privileged white women to pursue a career or leisure interests find it hard to make common cause with those white women in a search for liberation. Their cautiousness is based not solely on past experience, but also on a suspicion that women's liberation will perpetuate privilege for upper- and middle-class white women at the expense of working-class black women.

This is not an unfounded fear. For example, the increasing number of women with children who choose to work outside the home has created a demand for day-care facilities. Parents are often unable or unwilling to pay high fees for such care, so center budgets are limited and salaries are modest. They often employ a high percentage of minority persons who have fewer job options and thus are willing to work for the lower wages. If the current pattern of underfinancing of day-care centers continues, economically privileged white women will be involved in a variation on the old theme. We will gain the freedom to engage in outside activities by shifting child-care responsibilities to poorly paid women—many of whom are from disadvantaged ethnic groups.

White feminists who address the question of work must consider the exploitation of women who earn wages as domestics and child-care workers. Feminists should insist that the skill and responsibility that child-care workers demonstrate be recognized and compensated accordingly. Feminists need to investigate the economics of day care more carefully. To what extent can families genuinely afford to pay for the services of well-paid day-care workers? To what extent do many families require assistance in meeting the cost of adequate child care? Feminists (white and black) ought to factor good salaries and appropriate fringe benefits into their cost figures when determining the amount of assistance that churches, corporations, other organizations, and government will have to provide in order

---

[18]Fannie Lou Hamer, "It's in Your Hands," in Lerner, *Black Women in White America*, 610.

[19]Patricia Robinson, "Poor Black Women," in Lerner, *Black Women in White America*, 600.

to meet the needs of American children. Feminists should state unequivocally that fairness demands that wage-earning private household workers receive vacation and sick pay and that legally mandated Social Security payments be made by their employers.

White feminists who speak of work as liberating are often middle- and upper-class women who envision work as professional work. We are, or imagine ourselves as, doctors, lawyers, social workers, teachers, and writers. Economically privileged white feminists should be working to ensure that black women who do not have access to similar educational and economic resources gain greater opportunities to do rewarding work.

Helping to enlarge black female access to creative, adequately paid work will be a challenge for white feminists. For example, at present, the number of black students in graduate and professional schools is dropping. Many black women are finding it hard to qualify for professional jobs, since they often lack the money necessary for long years of required training. Economically privileged white feminists need to support programs, especially financial aid programs, that help economically disadvantaged black women get professional training.

The role of rewarding work as as one aspect of a full human life for all women is still a very open question for feminists—in both theory and practice. As feminists continue to explore this question, those of us who are white feminists need to pay careful attention to the interconnections between racism and sexism in women's experiences of work.

Female/Male Solidarity

Black and white feminists also have differing perspectives and priorities about the issue of male/female solidarity. Many black women were initially suspicious of the women's liberation movement because they believed women's liberation divided human beings into two opposing camps—oppressed women and oppressing men. Almost all black women refused to see themselves as involved in a struggle for liberation *over against* black men. Black women experienced themselves as joint members of an oppressed group: the black race in white America. Black women saw themselves as drawing strength from an alliance with black men in a historic struggle for black liberation.

In 1970 Inez Smith Reid conducted a series of interviews with black women selected because they exhibited insightful, effective, and deep commitments to end racial oppression. She questioned them about their attitudes toward the newly emerging women's liberation movement. These black women frequently expressed a concern that black women's participation in women's liberation would drive a wedge into the black community, weakening it in the struggle against racism.

Given the history of Black people in an oppressive and racist society many Black women now insist on the need for Black men and women to rebuild the kind of strong interpersonal links which would permit the Black male and the Black female to engage in a concerted thrust for Black liberation. Can Black women realistically add their strength to women's lib and still hope to unite with Black men in a constant and persistent struggle for Black liberation?[20]

Middle- or upper-class white feminists, on the other hand, rarely had the experience of struggling *together with* men to overcome a common oppression. We perceived men as privileged persons who monopolized opportunities for economic, political, and cultural fulfillment. We demanded a share in the public power that men possessed. We realized that privileged white men had larger public opportunities because they drew upon the private energies that women expended in child rearing and housekeeping and as "support" staff in the workplace. White male professionals and managers were able to pursue rewarding careers because we assumed the overwhelming share of family responsibilities (sometimes with the help of black domestics). We found that to demand access to public privileges and power entailed demanding that men share private burdens more equitably.

Angela Davis contends that black families have a different heritage. During the time of slavery, she argues, black men shared in the responsibilities of family maintenance in a manner unknown in the white community. According to Davis, slave women and men were equal partners in the field and in the cabin.

> Slave men executed important domestic responsibilities and were not, therefore . . . the mere helpmates of their women. For while women cooked and sewed, for example, men did the gardening and hunting. . . . This sexual division of domestic labor does not appear to have been hierarchical: men's tasks were certainly not superior to and were hardly inferior to the work performed by women. They were both equally necessary. Moreover, from all indications, the division of labor between the sexes was not always so rigorous, for men would sometimes work in the cabin and women might tend the garden and perhaps even join the hunt.[21]

Black women responded coolly toward feminism because it seemed to cast all men in the role of oppressor. Many black women responded that they were partners in the home and in the world struggling with black men

---

[20]Inez Smith Reid, *'Together' Black Women* (New York: Emerson Hall Publishers, 1972) 53.

[21]Davis, *Women, Race, and Class,* 17-18. E. Frances White disputes this description of gender roles in slave families. See "Listening to the Voices of Black Feminism," *Radical America* 18 (1984): 19-20.

against the evil of racism. Many black women—especially those who held jobs that provided little opportunity for creativity and that paid inadequate wages—found it nearly impossible to identify with white housewives who lamented their own constricted social position. Many black women pointed to their economic contribution as proof that black women were more equal in black families than many white women were in white marriages. Angela Davis describes this experience when she says that black women, who were rarely full-time housewives, escaped debilitating dependence on men. Thus, black women never learned the "alleged virtues" of "feminine weakness and wifely submissiveness."[22]

Although black feminists had many criticisms to voice about black and white men, they found that early accounts from a largely white women's movement seldom provided an adequate analysis of sexism as black women experienced it. Outspoken black feminists began to develop their own critique of sexist black male behavior in their own language. In voicing this critique, black feminists drew on a long tradition of black female solidarity. They remembered how their mothers and other women cautioned them about the failings of black men. One black scholar did a survey among her black students and found that the attitude toward men that many black women learned from older women was typified by the proverb: "Every man has some dog in him."[23] Black men were said to be unreliable and especially unfaithful, but heterosexual women still needed men as sexual partners. Black women began to question the price they paid for black male approval and affection.

Black women severely criticized black men for refusing them access to decision-making power in black groups. Toni Cade reported, "It would seem that every organization that you can name has had to struggle at one time or another with seemingly mutinous cadres of women getting salty about having to man the telephones or fix coffee while men wrote the position papers and decided on policy."[24] Black women denounced sexism in the rhetoric of the Black Power movement. They rejected the notion that a woman's place was exclusively behind her man supporting and nurturing his battered male ego while simultaneously bearing many (male) babies who would become the next generation of warriors.

Black feminists reassessed their family roles. While black women made important economic contributions to their families, they began to see that they were also doing almost all the family maintenance tasks. Black women

---

[22]Davis, *Women, Race, and Class*, 231.

[23]Gloria I. Joseph and Jill Lewis, *Common Differences: Conflicts in Black and White Feminist Perspectives* (Garden City NY: Doubleday, Anchor Press, 1981) 113.

[24]Toni Cade, "On the Issue of Roles," in *The Black Woman: An Anthology* (New York: New American Library, 1970) 107.

worked, kept the house, and raised the children. "Interestingly, the high percentage of unemployment among Black males has not resulted in Black males playing nurturance/mothering roles to any substantive degree. Sexism has severely influenced male attitudes toward roles in the home."[25] Black women began to realize the toll it takes when they do double duty in the work force and in the home. Institutional racism makes that double burden particularly heavy for black women who struggle to raise healthy children in a society that treats them as inferior, to console men battle-scarred from the fight against racism, and often, to do all this with few economic resources.

Black women began to see parallels between their own experience of oppression as women in the black community and the broadening, deepening analysis of sexism offered by the women's liberation movement. While some black women publicly voiced serious reservations about the fittingness of women's liberation ideas and tactics for black women's lives, a growing number of black women supported women's rights. In 1972 a Louis Harris Virginia Slims poll revealed that while only thirty-five percent of white women were sympathetic to women's liberation groups, sixty-seven percent of black women were.[26] More and more black women began identifying themselves publicly as feminists. Nonetheless, black feminists were clear that they needed to struggle simultaneously on at least two fronts: within the black community, to confront the sexism of black men, and, in solidarity with black men, to confront the reality of racism.

A dramatic statement of black women's unique attitude toward solidarity with men is found in the 1977 statement of the Combahee River Collective, a black lesbian feminist group from Boston.

> Although we are feminists and lesbians we feel solidarity with progressive Black men and do not advocate the fractionalization that white women who are separatists demand. Our situation as Black people necessitates that we have solidarity around the fact of race. . . . We struggle together with Black men against racism, while we also struggle with Black men about sexism.[27]

These black lesbian feminists explicitly rejected a feminist separatism that equates all oppression with sexual oppression and fails fully to comprehend the reality that black women *and men* are victims of shared racial oppression.

---

[25]Joseph and Lewis, *Common Differences*, 82.

[26]Hooks, *Ain't I a Woman*, 148.

[27]Combahee River Collective, "A Black Feminist Statement," in *This Bridge Called My Back: Writings by Radical Women of Color*, ed. Cherrie Moraga and Gloria Anzaldua (Watertown MA: Persephone Press, 1981) 213.

Some heterosexual black women have a special motive for resisting a women's liberation movement that may seem to set men and women at odds. Many heterosexual black women have greater difficulty in establishing satisfying long-term relationships with black men than heterosexual white women do with white men. By all statistical accounts, there are many fewer black men in their prime adult years than there are black women.[28] Therefore, it is often difficult for heterosexual black women to find black sexual partners. Because heterosexual black women sometimes have greater difficulty establishing good, long-lasting sexual relationships with black men, some heterosexual black women find it hard to make common cause with heterosexual white women who could be competitors for black male attention.

During the Freedom Summers of 1964 and 1965, when large numbers of white female civil rights volunteers worked in the black community, this tension was especially strong. Both young blacks and whites were testing the social boundaries for interracial relationships. Some white women engaged willingly, some less willingly, in sexual relations with black men. Some heterosexual black women became alienated and angry.[29] A fictional account of this tension is presented in the novel *Meridian*. The main characters are a black woman, a black man, and a white woman. The black woman, who is the title character, is bitterly hurt when her black lover begins dating white women. The narrator reports, "It was strange and unfair, but the fact that he dated them—and *so obviously because their color made them interesting*—made her ashamed, *as if she were less.*"[30] Some black women feel insulted when black men pursue white women because they are white. It is a special hurt when some black men seem to confirm the racist social ideal that white women *because of their racial characteristics* are more beautiful and desirable.

While the tension between heterosexual black women and heterosexual white women was particularly intense during the civil rights and Black Power movements, it continues into the present. Yet this tension should not be exaggerated. Pitting women in competition for male approval has been a major tactic for separating women from one another in a sexist society. To the extent that some women are divided from one another by

---

[28]Critics of the United States Census Bureau contend that black males, who have a highly mobile lifestyle that is incompatible with data-gathering methods tied to dwelling units, are drastically undercounted. There may be more young black men than census figures show. Nevertheless, homicide, suicide, disease, drug abuse, and incarceration take a high toll among black men.

[29]See Sara Evans, *Personal Politics: The Roots of Women's Liberation in the Civil Rights Movement and the New Left* (New York: Vintage Books, 1979) 78-82.

[30]Alice Walker, *Meridian* (New York: Washington Square Press, 1976) 106 (emphasis added).

heterosexual jealousy, our power to challenge institutional sexism is diminished. White feminists should neither overemphasize the black woman,
white woman, black man triangle nor ignore a potential division between
some white and black women that could weaken women's struggles for
justice.[31]

If the feminist movement is to be a movement that genuinely repre-
sents all women, its ideas must be varied and complex enough to illuminate the differing situations of all women. Feminist separatism is not a
viable political philosophy for most black women. Those of us who are
white feminists need to be careful that we do not articulate limited strategies for dealing with sexism as if they were the *only* legitimate feminist
strategies. White feminist separatist theories or strategies that ignore the
strong bond forged between many black women and men in a shared
struggle against racism do not speak to all women's experience.

Female Beauty and Self-Esteem

Heterosexual black women have suffered because white women have
been idealized as unattainable and especially enticing sex partners for black
men. Black women have also suffered because a particular, idealized image of the white woman has been held up as *the* ideal of female beauty. A
particular white woman—curvaceous in a distinctively Caucasian fashion,
usually blond and blue-eyed—has been held up as the American aesthetic
ideal for *all* women. In a racist society, black women are told from a young
age that they are ugly to the degree that they fail to conform to a white
standard. Black author Abbey Lincoln laments, "We are the women whose
hair is compulsively fried, whose skin is bleached, whose nose is 'too big,'
whose mouth is 'too big and loud,' whose behind is 'too big and broad,'
whose feet are 'too big and flat,' whose face is 'too black and shiny.'"[32]

The psychological experience of generations of black girls taught to
feel that they were hopelessly ugly is powerfully evoked in black literature. Poet Maya Angelou begins her autobiography remembering a day
when she wanted to be beautiful, admired, and loved. She described her
hopes as she anticipated reciting a poem for the children's section of the
Colored Methodist Episcopal Church. Contemplating the silk dress her
grandmother had altered for the occasion she exalted, "I knew that once
I put it on I'd look like a movie star. . . . I was going to look like one of *the
sweet little white girls who were everybody's dream of what was right with the world.*"

---

[31]There are also sexual tensions between black and white lesbians. Another facet
of the interstructured reality of oppression is the intertwining of sexism, heterosexism, and racism. For one view of these tensions, see Audre Lorde, *Zami: A New
Spelling of My Name* (Trumansburg NY: Crossing Press, 1982).

[32]Abbey Lincoln, "Who Will Revere the Black Woman?" in Cade, *The Black
Woman*, 84.

But when Easter morning dawned Angelou realized the cut-down dress she was to wear was ugly. She felt the faded color made her skin look like mud and imagined that everyone was staring at her skinny legs. In her humiliation Angelou indulged in her ultimate revenge fantasy.

> Wouldn't they be surprised when one day I woke out of my black ugly dream, and my real hair, which was long and blond, would take the place of the kinky mass that Momma wouldn't let me straighten? My light-blue eyes were going to hypnotize them. . . . [Then they would discover] I was really white and . . . a cruel fairy stepmother, who was understandably jealous of my beauty, had turned me into a too-big Negro girl, with nappy black hair, broad feet and a space between her teeth that would hold a number-two pencil.[33]

Black women have been taught by society to despise their own bodies. Advertising and entertainment media are among the most powerful tools for conveying white society's message that black women are ugly. Black women are often excluded completely from advertising and entertainment. When black women are permitted to appear, the models or actresses are often selected with an eye toward their similarity to the white women powerful white people deem beautiful. This is not equally true for black men. One group of black women who monitored advertising in which black models appeared concluded, "The males were not presented as copies of White males. Black males in the ads looked like your ordinary, everyday Black male, sufficiently handsome without White features or White hair texture. . . . Their Negroid features and Afro hairdos are cultivated, not altered."[34] In contrast, black female models had straight hair, light skin, and features that resembled the Caucasian. Black women find their self-esteem assaulted by omnipresent suggestions that black beauty is a contradiction in terms. Black women victimized by racist standards for beauty know that liberation for them must mean the power to destroy such notions and to claim their own bodies as beautiful.

The feminist movement, from its early demonstrations against the Miss America pageant to its continuing attacks upon the image of women in the media, has criticized a monolithic (and uniformly white) image of female beauty in American society.[35] Those of us who are white feminists need to continue to articulate clearly our critique of this monolithic ideal of beauty, including specific denunciations of its destructive impact on

---

[33]Maya Angelou, *I Know Why the Caged Bird Sings* (New York: Bantam Books, 1969) 1 (emphasis added), 2.

[34]Joseph and Lewis, *Common Differences,* 162.

[35]"No More Miss America!" in *Sisterhood is Powerful,* ed. Robin Morgan (New York: Vintage Books, 1970) 586.

black women and girls. We need to voice unmistakably a rejection of standards of female beauty that make one narrow white image the benchmark against which all women are judged.

White feminists have a responsibility to learn about black women's perspectives on women's issues, to analyze how racist social structures may distort the impact of white feminist proposals, and to support black women in their self-defined struggle for liberation. Black feminists are creating their own analyses of sexism and of the interconnections between racism and sexism. Black feminists reject those white feminist theories that equate all oppression with sexual oppression and that cannot encompass black women's multifaceted experience of oppression. White feminist theologians who are seeking to contribute to an inclusive feminist theology that respects and reflects the diversity of women's experience need to learn from the experiences of black women.

6 | Racism and Feminist Theology

WHITE FEMINIST RACISM is evident when we describe our own limited experience as if it were universal female experience and ignore the distinctive experiences of black women. Those of us who are white feminists also display racism when we establish priorities or select strategies for our own struggle against sexism without sufficiently examining the importance of those priorities for, or the impact of those strategies on, the black community. We perpetuate racism in the movement when we act as if white women alone were wise enough to set the agenda, distribute the resources, and create new visions for the women's movement.

Feminist theology should be a resource that helps religiously oriented feminists deal with racism. Yet even white feminist theologians who are struggling with our own racism fail, at times, to understand and acknowledge the distinctive experiences of black women. Some white feminist theologians also proclaim a new version of the True Womanhood myth, which threatens to obscure white women's moral fallibility in a racist society. Nonetheless, in our better moments, many white feminist theologians are struggling to confront racism honestly, to analyze the complex interconnections between racism and sexism, to acknowledge the moral fallibility of white women, and to create communities of accountability committed to the struggle against sexism, racism, and all other forms of human oppression.

Acknowledging Black Women's Experience

White feminist theologians are tempted to treat our own white experience as if it were universal and to render black experience invisible. White feminist theologians need to engage in the constant discipline of analyzing our experience as *white* experience and stating explicitly how our experience appears to differ from that of black women.

Feminist theologian Rosemary Ruether has been in the forefront among feminist theologians who have insisted that racism must be a major priority. She has produced particularly illuminating analyses of the interconnections between racism and sexism.[1] Yet even Ruether can slip into

[1]Ruether has written about racism many times. Two of her more detailed

the trap of speaking from a position of relative privilege without explicitly aknowledging that black women do not have access to the same opportunities.

When discussing the future of feminist theology in the academic world, Ruether acknowledges that she speaks from "a white Western Christian context," and she calls for an inclusive feminist theology that must emerge out of "a network of solidarity" existing among many feminist communities "engaged in the critique of patriarchalism in distinct cultural and religious contexts," rather than "one dominant form of feminism that claims to speak for the whole of womankind." Yet Ruether emphasizes the increasing numbers of women students in theological schools and lauds the "enormous amount of solid work in all fields [of feminist theology] that has been accomplished in these past fifteen years." However, she does not remind her audience that the work has been done by and on behalf of *white* women.[2] Black women are a tiny percentage among the graduate students in religion; they are an even smaller percentage of the faculties in departments of religion and seminaries. Black women have had few opportunities for sustained theological reflection upon their religious experience. As yet, there is no "enormous amount" of *published* work on *black* feminist theology.

Ruether raises a critical question for feminist theology: what institutional bases are available to serve as the platform from which feminists can project our visions of the future? She contends that feminists must make use of established theological institutions as one base, since these institutions are among the few platforms that can be seized. She declares that as men's daughters, mothers, and sisters, feminists can legitimately claim a share of their resources.[3] But, uncharacteristically, Ruether does not acknowledge that it is *white* women who are the sisters and daughters of the men who control most of the wealthier and more powerful religious institutions; it is not black fathers and brothers who control the American Academy of Religion (which Ruether was addressing). To claim a share as sisters and daughters in the Divinity School at Howard University is a far

---

treatments of the topic are "Between the Sons of Whites and the Sons of Blackness: Racism and Sexism in America," in *New Woman/New Earth: Sexist Ideologies and Human Liberation* (New York: Seabury Press, 1975) 115-33, and "Crisis in Sex and Race: Black Theology vs. Feminist Theology," *Christianity and Crisis* 34 (15 April 1974): 67-73.

[2] Rosemary Ruether, "Feminist Theology: On Becoming the Tradition," *Christianity and Crisis* 45 (4 March 1985): 58. My attention was drawn to this article by comments upon it by black theologian Delores Williams. I share some, but not all of, Williams's criticisms of the piece. "The Color of Feminism," *Christianity and Crisis* 45 (29 April 1985): 164-65.

[3] Ruether, "Feminist Theology," 61.

different matter than to demand a new division of the resources of the Divinity School at Harvard University.

In her classic work, *Beyond God the Father*, Mary Daly also ignores black women's experience when she names her theological method, "liberation-castration-exorcism." She takes a term—castrating bitch—that has been used pejoratively as a weapon against assertive women and turns it into a positive theological term. Castration becomes the method whereby women unmask and destroy dehumanizing, masculine images of God that serve to legitimate patriarchy.[4] Thus Daly transforms the word "castrating" from a tool of patriarchal domination into a name for liberating female iconoclasm. However, in the process she never discusses differences in the way accusations of castration have been used under *racist* patriarchy to control black women.

Black women have suffered from the epithet, "castrating bitch," in a special way. They have been condemned for strength developed in the fight for survival in a racist society. Black women have frequently been forced to bear heavy economic burdens. Since the Civil War white men and women have been increasingly willing to give working-class and poor black women certain menial work, while many working-class and poor black men remain unemployed or underemployed. Black women have long provided important economic support for many black families. In a society that punished black male assertiveness harshly, black women have sometimes been able to be more forthright and assertive in their relationships with white people. Black women, who were sometimes permitted a limited economic base and social voice denied to black men, were labeled as voracious matriarchs—the castrators of their black men—by white critics.

Moreover, frustrated black men sometimes derided the black woman as "Sapphire," the dominating, castrating bitch. Toni Cade asserts that, even in the modern Black Power movement, women were demeaned on the basis of the old Sapphire stereotypes.

> And there is a dangerous trend observable in some quarters of the Movement to program Sapphire out of her "evil" ways into a cover up, shut up, lay-back-and-be-cool obedience role. She is being assigned an unreal role of mute servant that supposedly neutralizes the acidic tension that exists between Black men and Black women. She is being encouraged—in the name of revolution no less—to cultivate "virtues" that if listed would sound like the personality traits of slaves.[5]

[4]Mary Daly, *Beyond God the Father* (Boston: Beacon Press, 1973) 19.

[5]Toni Cade, "On the Issue of Roles," in *The Black Woman: An Anthology*, ed. Toni Cade (New York: New American Library, 1970) 102.

Many black women dispute the allegation that they have emasculated their men by assuming matriarchal power. They reject advice that they should resume a properly subservient "womanly" role in order to restore the manhood of black males.

> In reality Black women, domineering or not, have not had the power in this male dominated culture to effect a coup against anyone's manhood—in spite of their oft-cited economic "advantage" over the Black man. A matriarchal system is one in which power rests firmly in the hands of women. We suggest that whatever economic power may accrue to Black women by way of the few employment escape valves permitted them by the oppressing group . . . , this power is really illusory. . . . American society is patriarchal—white women suffer the slings and arrows of the system in the first instance. Black women are victimized on two counts: they are women and they are Black.[6]

In her early work Mary Daly was acutely sensitive to the suffering of strong white women who have been labeled "castrating bitches," but she ignored the distinctive contours of the black woman's experience with such insults. She also ignored black women's bonds with black men, for whom the term also holds a special meaning. For a long time after Emancipation, white terrorists used vicious sexual mutilation as a tactic to deny black people a legitimate share of economic resources and political power. Black men who stood up for the rights of their people had to live with the risk of real, physical castration.

Castration was a term of terror for black women, too. Black women have many close relationships with men. They are mothers, aunts, wives, lovers, sisters, nieces, and/or daughters of black men. Black women who had male loved ones lived in dread that the men for whom they cared would be castrated. Thus, the term that Daly chose to highlight in *Beyond God the Father* is the very term that reminds black women of the awful vulnerability of their fathers, brothers, and/or sons. Daly, in speaking of castration, failed to see the double jeopardy of black women—condemned for an imaginary emasculation of black men and living with the fear of real castration of black men by white terrorists.[7]

---

[6]Jean Carey Bond and Patricia Peery, "Is the Black Male Castrated?" in Cade, *The Black Woman*, 116-17.

[7]In *Gyn/ecology* and *Pure Lust* Daly uses the word *castration* to denote the dismemberment of women's bodies, minds, and/or spirits or to describe men's destructive, deforming efforts to cut women off from biophilic potency/power. Hence, in these works *castration* is used as a negative term. While even this usage ignores the concrete historical experience of the black community, the fact that the word is not used as a positive term renders its utilization less problematic. For example, see *Gyn/ecology: The Metaethics of Radical Feminism* (Boston: Beacon Press, 1978) 227, and *Pure Lust: Elemental Feminist Philosophy* (Boston: Beacon Press, 1984) 166-70.

In her recent *Pure Lust,* Daly again fashions a mirror for women's experience without sufficient attention to how it will reflect the experience of black women. Daly celebrates the Race of Lusty Women, which, in turn, participates in the Race of Elemental Be-ing, that is, in nature, the Earth, and the cosmos. She claims woman-identified women "choose this our own Race of Elemental Be-ing over all man-made, male designed divisions and categories." Daly contends that patriarchy shuts women off from the deepest sources of female power. Women are "cut off from knowledge of our Race's customs and traditions."[8]

But only culturally privileged white women (those whose primary focus is on sexism) are likely to feel such unambiguous loyalty to the Race of Women. White women who are the heirs to certain European cultures that, in turn, shape the dominant white culture within the United States can take our racial heritage for granted. Our own white customs and traditions are so dominant that these cultural patterns become our *unexamined social horizon*. Thus, we might articulate only a longing for knowledge of the traditions of the Race of Women.

A *black* feminist woman, on the other hand, is likely to identify with the black race as well as the Race of Lusty Women. Indeed, she may well be more reluctant or ambivalent about bonding with white women in the Race of Lusty Women than about bonding with her black brothers. A woman who is of African and/or Caribbean descent may mean something quite different when she laments the loss her race's customs and traditions. She might also long for knowledge of, or social recognition and esteem for, a culture and traditions *which she shares with men of her ethnic background.*[9]

Apparently, Daly does not sufficiently appreciate the complex reverberations the word *race* may set off in the minds and hearts of black women.[10] When Daly asserts, "Those whose Race has been labeled, maimed, killed, and dismembered as 'evil' cannot be dispassionate about evil," she uses *race* to refer to women. The maiming and killing she has in

---

[8]Daly, *Pure Lust,* 5, 6. Daly views racist divisions as one of the horrors of man-made society. To participate truly in women's movement into a future free of patriarachy is, therefore, to move to eradicate racist divisions.

[9]Women from non-dominant ethnic groups, such as Polish women, Filipino women, Lebanese women, and women from working-class cultures might also yearn for knowledge of traditions they share with their men. This is also true for Jewish women.

[10]Daly chooses the word *race* because it connotes not just women as a new people or nation, but also the movement of women as they create new futures. Women are rushing foward as in a race; they course through narrow channels like a "race" or current of water. My discussion of the Race of Lusty Women fails to convey Daly's sense of urgent motion and hence risks freezing her kinetic term, "making it almost dull enough to be a suitable topic for an 'alternative' Sunday sermon." Daly, *Pure Lust,* 407.

mind is violence against women, especially the witchcraft persecutions. But a black woman could not read that sentence in such one-dimensional terms; for her, races—the race of women and the black race—have *both* "been labeled, maimed, killed, and dismembered as evil."[11]

Black poet Audre Lorde warns white feminists about another failure in naming. White feminists often overlook those aspects of black female experience that provide *positive, powerful images for all women.* When speaking of the Goddess as a source of power, we frequently name only Indo-European Goddess figures. Lorde asks where the black Goddesses are. "Where was Afrekete, Yemanje, Oyo, and Mawulisa? Where are the warrior-goddesses of the Vodun, the Dohomeian Amazons and warrior-women of Dan?" Although Lorde knows that including material about black women's spiritual heritage is difficult, especially since little has been written about the topic from a feminist perspective, she contends that to exclude black women's spiritual history from a discussion of women's connection to Being "is to deny the fountain of non-european female strength and power that nurtures each of our visions."[12]

In *Pure Lust* it is clear that Mary Daly has heard and responded positively to such criticism. She does use strong black women as sources of wisdom for all women. She draws upon and celebrates the words and actions of black women such as Harriet Tubman, Sojourner Truth, Flo Kennedy, and Alice Walker. Nor does she fall into the trap of allowing black women to speak only about racial oppression: she quotes Alice Walker on fighting nuclear madness; she ponders the lives of two black female characters from *Sula,* a novel by black writer Toni Morrison, in order to probe the meaning of genuine female friendship; and she welcomes Alice Walker's wisdom about cosmic power expressed in the words of Walker's character Shug Avery from the novel, *The Color Purple*—"It [God] ain't nothing you can look at apart from anything else, including yourself." Although Daly rarely uses Goddess language in *Pure Lust,* when she does speak of the Goddess, Daly names Egyptian/African Goddesses, Isis and Seka(u)it, along with Indo-European ones. In addition, she discusses the Black Madonnas found throughout Europe, probes their identification with fertility and the earth, and "wonders" about possible Egyptian/African sources for the Black Madonnas.[13]

If white feminist theologians are to contribute to the creation of new theologies that reflect the diversity of human experience, we must admit

---

[11]Daly, *Pure Lust,* 270.

[12]Audre Lorde, "An Open Letter to Mary Daly," in *This Bridge Called My Back: Writings by Radical Women of Color,* ed. Cherrie Moraga and Gloria Anzaldua (Watertown MA: Persephone Press, 1981) 94, 95.

[13]Daly, *Pure Lust,* 351-52, 379-81, 402, 116-20.

the particularity of our own experience. Those of us who are white feminists need to inform ourselves about and to acknowledge *explicitly* the diverse experiences of black women. As Mary Daly's work in *Pure Lust* shows, white feminists can grow and be enriched by listening to the voices of black women.

Connections Between Racism and Sexism

Sexism as the Primary Evil

White feminist theologians frequently describe sexism as the original sin upon which all other forms of human (and ecological) exploitation are modeled. This is an oversimplified model of human oppression. Reliance on such an inadequate model can obscure the sins committed by racially privileged women.

According to Mary Daly, patriarchy is "the perverted paradigm and source of other social evils." It is "the most basic, radical, and universal social manifestation of evil, . . . underlying not only rapism but also racism."[14] Given Daly's view of the interrelationship between racism and sexism, the ending of sexism must take priority. Daly believes that the end of sexism—the primordial form of oppression—will spell the end of racism. She fears that black men freed from racial oppression would continue to oppress women by perpetuating sexist values and structures. It is clear to Daly that men fighting for black liberation are not always committed to the liberation of all women, or even to the full liberation of black women. Therefore she cautions black women against giving their full loyalty to a black liberation movement that fixes its attention upon "some deformity *within* patriarchy . . . rather than patriarchy itself, without recognizing sexism as root and paradigm of the various forms of oppression . . . [it seeks] to eradicate."[15]

Daly doubts that black liberation would result in equal dignity and freedom for black women, but she is far more sanguine about the result of women's liberation. She believes that the liberation of women implies the liberation of all persons, especially persons suffering racial oppression. Daly pictures sexism as the foundation of a structure of other social oppressions, including racism. She suggests that abolishing sexism would cause its racist superstructure to topple automatically.

Feminist theologian and biblical scholar, Elisabeth Schüssler Fiorenza, offers a somewhat more complex analysis of the relationship between racism and sexism. Schüssler Fiorenza contends that patriarchy is a pyramidal structure with heavier burdens of injustice borne by women from the "lower" races, ethnic groups, and/or classes. Not all women are equally

---

[14]Ibid., xii, 164.

[15]Daly, *Beyond God the Father*, 56.

oppressed. Rather, patriarchy is a structure "of graded subordinations and exploitations [which] specifies women's oppression in terms of the class, race, country, or religion of the men to whom we 'belong.' " Schüssler Fiorenza believes that patriarchal oppression serves as the paradigm for modes of oppression in which men exploit *other men.* "Patriarchy defines not just women as the 'other' but also subjugated peoples and races as the 'other' to be dominated." This sentence is unfortunately phrased, since it obscures women among subjugated peoples and races. However, Schüssler Fiorenza quickly acknowledges that poor women and women of color are doubly or triply oppressed under such a system. In fact, her pyramidal analysis of patriarchal oppression leads her to give special emphasis to the plight of women at the bottom of the pyramid, whose double and triple suffering is most severe. According to Schüssler Fiorenza, patriarchy finds its fullest expression in the crushing exploitation of those women who are poorest and most socially despised. The forces that dehumanize women at the bottom reveal the "full death-dealing power of patriarchy."[16] Unfortunately, Schüssler Fiorenza does not extend her pyramidal metaphor to explore explicitly how women located in the higher tiers put stress on the women and men below them.

To the extent that feminist theologians name sexism as the primary manifestation of evil—the paradigm for all other oppressions, we risk an oversimplified identification of human oppressions. A model of sexism as the foundation for all other oppressions or as a pyramid of graded oppressions has important limitations. It does not adequately suggest the social, structural interconnections among modes of oppression. Such models tend to obscure the extent to which people who are oppressed also participate in the oppression of others. White women participate in institutional racism; black men, in institutional sexism.

Reducing racism to a subsidiary manifestation of patriarchy can also lead to premature identification of white women's interests with the interests of all subjugated peoples. Such models of the interrelationships among oppressions allow those of us who are privileged white feminists to legitimate the pursuit of our own interests without examining the impact of our actions on other oppressed persons. It permits us to believe that what benefits us is conveniently in the best interests of all the oppressed.

The Interstructuring of Oppressions

In *New Woman/New Earth* Rosemary Ruether offered a more adequate social analysis. She described racism and sexism as interstructured.

In fact, racism and sexism have been closely interrelated historically, especially in the American South, but they have not been ex-

---

[16]Elisabeth Schüssler Fiorenza, *Bread Not Stone: The Challenge of Feminist Biblical Interpretation* (Boston: Beacon Press, 1984) xiv, 5, xv.

actly parallel. Rather, we should recognize them as interstructural elements of oppression within the overarching system of white male domination. But this interstructuring of oppression by sex, race and also class, creates intermediate tensions and alienations—between white and black women, between black men and white women, and even between black men and black women.[17]

Racism and sexism are not just parallel columns both supporting the weight of white male privilege.

Extending Ruether's image, I suggest that racism and sexism are more like the steel girders of a skyscraper. Some girders run parallel supporting weight from above, but other girders run horizontally sustaining the vertical supports. In the same way, racial and sexual oppression sometimes run parallel absorbing comparable strains from the dominant white male class. But racism and sexism also run horizontally—intersecting each other. Black men participate in and support sexist structures that benefit them. White women participate in and support racist structures that benefit them. Black women absorb stress from both directions because they stand at the intersection of both racism and sexism.

Ruether warns that those of us who are white feminists must give explicit attention to the ways we are involved in race and class privilege. If we do not, we risk social encapsulation; our feminist theories only articulate privileged white women's aspirations to share the social prerogatives of white men. "Any women's movement which is *only* concerned about sexism and not other forms of oppression, must remain a women's movement of the white upper class, for it is *only* this group of women whose *only* problem is the problem of being women, since in every other way, they belong to the ruling class."[18] Unless we give careful attention to the realities of race and class, privileged white women (who are speaking only of our own needs and dreams) may imagine that we speak for all women.

Moreover, white women's groups that do not give explicit attention to the realities of race and class will find that we can be manipulated by dominant males who appeal to unexamined class and race interests. For example, economically privileged white women who have paying jobs are increasingly demanding relief from the double burden of work on the job and at home. Well-to-do white males can evade this demand for a more equitable division of household duties by providing money to pay household workers from economically exploited racial and ethnic groups. As Ruether warns, white feminists who are unaware of race and class issues

---

[17]Ruether, *New Woman/New Earth,* 116.

[18]Ibid., 125.

might "disregard [our] ties with other oppressed groups" and cooperate in a "strategy for consolidating the power of the ruling class and race."[19]

Ruether alerts white women to the possibility that privileged males may be able to use us to shore up existing race and class structures. However, we are not just the victims of white male manipulation. We are active moral agents who can and do make our own choices to perpetuate or to resist structures from which we, as whites, draw unfair benefits.

Economics

Feminists must address economic issues if the gains of the women's movement are to be more than just an extension of unjust white upper-class male privilege to a few upper-class white women.

> Without creating the socioeconomic conditions for equality, the rights earned by feminists remain middle-class privileges for those women who are either childless or who can afford to pay a house-keeper and nursemaid. The vast majority of women will remain tied to their traditional caste roles as the auxiliary support system of male work, both at home and on the job.[20]

Feminist theologians need to develop a more comprehensive and nuanced economic dimension in our social analysis—one more fully descriptive of the interstructuring of sexism, racism, and economic exploitation. Work in this essential area is, in some sense, just beginning. It is no wonder that the feminist theologians who participated in a recent project on theological education say, "nothing has been as difficult for us to talk about as economic injustice."[21] We do not yet have the intellectual tools we need to explore fully the interconnections between race, sex, and class. Nor have we examined our own experiences of class in sufficient depth.

Feminist theologians have criticized the social privilege of economically advantaged men who monopolize opporutnities for creative labor while relegating a host of menial tasks to underpaid, or unpaid, and undervalued women (and socially disadvantaged men). As sociologist Michele Russell told the Theology in the Americas Conference, most of the wage labor that is available to women replicates our subservient roles in the home. "We find ourselves concentrated in the sectors of the economy that . . . are the public, institutionalized extensions of long-standing

---

[19]Rosemary R. Ruether, "Response," *Women's Caucus—Religious Studies Newsletter* 2 (Winter 1974): 6.

[20]Ruether, *New Woman/New Earth*, 179-80.

[21]The Mudflower Collective, *God's Fierce Whimsy: Christian Feminism and Theological Education* (New York: Pilgrim Press, 1985) 77.

domestic roles: waitresses, laundresses, nurses, cooks, sales clerks, seam-stresses, teachers, maids, producers of non-durable consumer goods."[22]

Feminist theologians have insisted that we need to reexamine the sep-aration between work and the home that characterizes advanced indus-trial societies. We have been particularly critical of the double burden that women must routinely assume when we work for wages. Women are ex-pected to perform all the tasks of men in comparable positions and to shoulder the major responsibility for household maintenance. In the ab-sence of social relief from this double burden, women remain concen-trated in underpaid clerical and service positions that can more easily be combined with heavy family responsibilities. Women will not be liberated until we are liberated from a mandatory double shift (at home and at work). Freeing women from this double shift cannot be left to the private ar-rangements of individual couples. A more just distribution of household responsibilities will require a reallocation of social resources and a trans-formation of the current patterns of work and so-called private life.[23]

It is important to explore the connections between white feminist dis-cussions of this double burden and the experiences of black women. His-torically, black women have borne the burden of the double shift much longer than middle-class white women. Two-earner, married-couple fam-ilies are still more common among blacks than among whites. In addition, there are a significant number of black women who support a household without a husband present. However, because black mothers without husbands tend to be younger, to have completed fewer years of school, and to have more children than their white counterparts, they are more often unemployed.[24] Black women have diverse experiences with the problem of combining job and household responsibilities. Their experi-ences are also somewhat different from those of their white peers. These

[22]Michele Russell, "Women, Work, and Politics in the U.S.," in *Theology in the Americas,* ed. Sergio Torres and John Eagleson (Maryknoll NY: Orbis Books, 1976) 344-45.

[23]Beverly Wildung Harrison, "The Effect of Industrialization on the Role of Women in Society," in *Making the Connections: Essays in Feminist Social Ethics,* ed. Carol S. Robb (Boston: Beacon Press, 1985) 42-53; Rosemary Radford Ruether, "Home and Work: Women's Roles and the Transformation of Values," in *Woman: New Dimensions,* ed. Walter Burkhardt (New York: Paulist Press, 1975) 71-83; and Barbara Hilkert Andolsen, "A Woman's Work Is Never Done: Unpaid Household Labor as a Social Justice Issue," in *Women's Consciousness, Women's Conscience,* ed. Barbara Hilkert Andolsen, Christine E. Gudorf, and Mary D. Pellauer (Minne-apolis: Winston/Seabury, 1985) 3-18.

[24]U.S. Department of Labor, Women's Bureau, *The United Nations Decade for Women, 1976-1985: Employment in the United States* (Washington DC: Government Printing Office, 1985) 23-28.

are differences that we should acknowledge and examine as we develop a more nuanced economic analysis.

Feminist theologians need to investigate the capacity of the national economy to respond to the material needs of diverse groups of women. Feminist ethicist Beverly Harrison warns that "our society is organized to ensure that everything that can be done with monetary profit will be done by so-called private enterprise and everything that cannot be turned into profit will be funded by the state, and underfunded because it is not profitable."[25] Services essential to the well-being of diverse groups of women are not available in a quantity and quality proportionate to our needs. Feminist ethicist Nancy Bancroft notes that in a "cutback economy" even the meager social services the state provides to wage earning women and others are scaled back or eliminated.[26]

Feminist theologians need to incorporate a global economic dimension into our social analysis. The interconnections between racism and sexism cannot be fully understood without connecting both to conditions within the international economic system. The world economy is currently under severe stress resulting from such factors as technological change, renewed international competition, shifts in patterns of production and consumption of natural resources, and international monetary pressures. In such uncertain and difficult economic times, it is harder to address the needs of women, particularly the needs of those who are doubly and triply oppressed.

We need to examine in detail how racism, sexism, and economic exploitation are interrelated in a world economy controlled by elite groups that make key economic decisions. But we must not be satisfied with a one-dimensional analysis of economic injustice that emphasizes only the sinfulness of some "other"—the economic elite. Our economic analysis must be complex enough to take into account the temptation, for persons at intermediate points in an interstructured unjust world economy, to try to shift stresses from themselves to other groups. Women who are more privileged by reason of race and/or class will be tempted to consolidate our shaky economic advantages on a short-term basis by supporting political and economic policies that increase the stresses experienced by less privileged women and men.

---

[25]Beverly Wildung Harrison, "The Older Person's Worth in the Eyes of Society," in *Making the Connections,* ed. Robb, 159.

[26]Nancy Bancroft, "Women in the Cutback Economy: Ethics, Ideology, and Class," in *Women's Consciousness, Women's Conscience,* ed. Andolsen, Gudorf, and Pellauer, 19-32.

A Dangerous New True Womanhood

An interstructured social analysis that explores the interconnections between sexism, racism, and economic exploitation alerts white women to the moral ambiguity of our situation. White women are oppressed *as women*, but we wield forms of social power as *whites* and, perhaps, as economically privileged persons. A renewed white feminist ideology of True Womanhood which includes the assumption that *all women* (or some select group of women) *as women* have higher moral sensitivities is dangerous because it obscures our moral accountability for racism.

This construction of a renewed myth of True Womanhood is most apparent in the work of certain theorists from the women's spirituality movement who assert that women are uniquely life affirming, peace loving, cooperative, poetic, intuitive, sensitive to human relationships, attuned to nature, and nurturing (not just of children but of themselves, other persons, and creative projects). Sally Gearhart claims that women are uniquely in tune with spiritual energy within themselves. She also believes that groups of women truly "present" to themselves and to each other have the potential to raise *womanpower*, which can save the human race and the earth from destruction. In a discussion of war and nuclear weapons, Barbara Zanotti proclaims, "Women are the bearers of lifeloving energy. Ours is the task of deepening that passion for life and separating from all that threatens life, . . . becoming who we are as women; . . . shifting the weight of the world." She concludes that the planet can be saved from patriarchal destruction only by those who break their ties with men who have deep violent proclivities—men for whom war creates the ultimate male bond. In *Beyond God the Father*, Mary Daly describes the "marginal situation of females in an androcentric world" as a morally superior vantage point. She pictures women as having been forced to the outermost edges of society. From the boundary, women have the clearest view of social injustice. They see most sharply what must be done in order to institute a just social order.[27]

Daly has a powerful point when she describes how women who are the targets of sexism can use our marginal position as a standpoint from which to understand and to take action against sexism. However, she does not explicitly acknowledge that women (and men) suffer from diverse forms of oppression. The boundary position of white feminists is a privileged

[27]Sally Gearhart, "Womanpower: Energy Re-Sourcement," in *The Politics of Women's Spirituality*, ed. Charlene Spretnak (Garden City NY: Doubleday, Anchor Press, 1982) 194-206; Barbara Zanotti, "Patriarchy: A State of War," in *Reweaving the Web of Life*, ed. Pam McAllister (Philadelphia: New Society, 1982) 19; Daly, *Beyond God the Father*, 32.

standpoint when the goal is to understand sexism, but it provides a much more limited perspective on racism.

In more recent work Daly displays great confidence in the woman-identified women who have increasingly become the focus of her work. She trusts the wisdom and moral passion of women who have had the courage to look into the vortex of patriarchal evil—with its whirling currents of gynecide, genocide, racism, ecological disaster, and nuclear destruction. As a whole, *Gyn/ecology* and *Pure Lust* create the impression that woman-identified women have experiences that make them impervious to the temptations to which men and male-identified women are prone.

Throughout her work, Daly implies that those white feminists who understand their own oppression clearly are able, by virtue of this self-understanding, to comprehend other forms of human subjection more adequately. She also conflates feminist understanding of the dynamics of racism based on its similarity to sexism with white feminist motivation to act vigorously to end racism. She glosses over the question, "What will motivate white women who benefit from racism to work for its end?"

Daly might question my assertion that white women benefit from racism. She tends to describe white women as standing on the boundary of the racist social institutions in this country. She suggests that white women have been so removed from centers of power and authority that they are not responsible for structures of racism. In *Beyond God the Father*, commenting on the hostility of certain Black Power advocates toward white women, she remonstrates, "yet it was not women who brought slaves to America. Women have been pawns in the racial struggle, which is basically not the struggle that will set them free as women." In *Pure Lust* Daly denounces "the *patriarchal* institutions of slavery and racism."[28]

Such heavy emphasis on the patriarchal dimensions of slavery obscures the moral responsibilities borne by those white women who participated in and perpetuated slavery. Some white women actively brutalized black slaves. Bell Hooks notes that white mistresses frequently failed to show compassion toward slave women, even, or perhaps especially, when the black women were raped by white masters. As an example, Hooks retells the story of one white woman who, upon discovering her husband in the act of raping a thirteen-year-old slave girl, had *the girl* imprisoned in a smokehouse and beaten repeatedly.[29]

In *Pure Lust* Daly faces squarely the reality of similar instances in which white women from slaveholding families failed to show compassion for brutally mistreated slave women or in which white women actually inflicted atrocities on slave women themselves. Daly does not draw back from

[28]Daly, *Beyond God the Father*, 57; Daly, *Pure Lust*, 378 (emphasis added).

[29]Bell Hooks, *Ain't I a Woman: Black Women and Feminism* (Boston: South End Press, 1981) 36-37.

acknowledging the "compound complicity involved when phallocratic [male controlled] racial oppression further desensitizes and dissociates the [white] woman who has 'power' from her more oppressed [black] sister." But Daly treats such white women as accomplices—"token torturers" who are "man-ipulated" by men who hold real institutional power. It is, therefore, men who bear real institutional responsibility for slavery. Daly emphasizes that white slave mistresses were trained for and sustained in their inhumanity by *patriarchal* religion, *patriarchal* marriage, and the *patriarchal* institutions of slavery and racism. "None of these institutions were invented by women or have ever been under the control of women."[30]

Daly oversimplifies the complexity of the moral responsibility of those more privileged white women *who are denied social control and power insofar as they are women, but who wield other forms of social control and power insofar as they are white and economically privileged*. White women, as the female relatives of slaveholders and as slaveholders in their own right, had real— often life and death—power over black slave women and men. White women may not have created the institution of slavery, but some of them took an active role in its maintenance. The example of white female abolitionists Angelina and Sarah Grimké shows that white women from slaveholding families did have a choice.[31] They could have actively resisted slavery, although at great personal cost. It is important to explore the patriarchal dimensions of white women's experience with the American slavery system. However, to focus too exclusively on slavery as a patriarchal institution without also analyzing it as a white institution is to flinch from looking at evil within the hearts of white women.

The issue of the moral complicity of white women is, of course, not merely a historic one. The question before us now is the moral complicity of white women in present-day structures of racism. Daly acknowledges that white women who are racially and economically privileged do have derivative social power. "As derivative beings, women share in some of the privileges and many of the hardships of their male possessors. For example, as white, wealthy or middle class, many women have advantages over many sisters in other echelons of the patriarchal world, as well as over many men of oppressed races, classes, nations, and other groups."[32] But Daly does not explore adequately the moral challenge confronting those of us white women who share with white men responsibility for racism.

Rosemary Ruether, on the other hand, helps white women to struggle with racism by challenging the myth of True Womanhood and cautioning

---

[30]Daly, *Pure Lust*, 376, 378.

[31]See Gerda Lerner, *The Grimké Sisters from South Carolina: Pioneers for Woman's Rights and Abolition* (New York: Schocken Books, 1967).

[32]Daly, *Pure Lust*, 240.

women about our own potential for moral evil. She insists that when women believe that we *as women* are more generous, life-affirming, and hence more morally upright than are men, we blind ourselves to the complexity of the moral choices all people face. Ruether recognizes that women can make no claims to a special moral purity. She criticizes any tendency to define one's own group as the moral elite.

> The Western apocalyptic model of liberation theology polarizes the world into "light" and "darkness," elect and damned, good and evil. Liberation movements draw on the same tendency to absolute polarity, but in a reverse form. To recognize structures of oppression within our own group would break up this model of ultimate righteousness and projection of guilt upon the "others." It would force us to deal with ourselves, not as simply oppressed or oppressors, but as people who are sometimes one and sometimes the other in different contexts. A more mature and chastened analysis of the capacities of human beings for good and evil would flow from this perception.[33]

Feminists run a dangerous risk when we proclaim a revised version of the myth that women are more moral than are men. Such a false dichotomy could well lull us into moral complacency. "If evil is male, then women don't have to take any responsibility for it."[34] Those of us who are white women must acknowledge our own capacity to do evil in order to face the fact that we participate in institutional racism.

Right Relations

The Moral Legitimacy of Self-Assertion

Concern for the evil done by white women poses in a new way the question that arose over the Fourteenth and Fifteenth Amendments to the Constitution. Is the assertion of group interest by economically comfortable white women morally legitimate? There is the risk, after all, that many strategies devised to obtain greater justice for women will benefit principally women like ourselves—women who share many of the privileges of dominant males.

The alternative would seem to be for white economically privileged women to assign highest priority to the interests of women who are "more severely oppressed." This position was advocated by black members of the Working Group on Racism/Classism/Sexism who met at the Women's Spirit Bonding Conference at Grailville in 1982. They proposed, "if it is

---

[33]Ruether, *New Woman/New Earth*, 132.

[34]Rosemary R. Ruether, "Goddesses and Witches: Liberation and Counter-Cultural Feminism," *Christian Century* 97 (10-17 September 1982): 844.

to be inclusive, the feminist movement must opt for a strategic, privileged focus on the agenda of Women of Color—Blacks, Hispanics, Asians and Indigenous Women."[35]

Such a strategic priority seems to me to be implicit also in Elisabeth Schüssler Fiorenza's pyramidal analysis of patriarchal oppression. She declares that "patriarchy cannot be toppled except when the women who form the bottom of the patriarchal pyramid, triply oppressed women, become liberated."[36] It would seem to follow, although Schüssler Fiorenza does not explicitly state this, that actions to liberate racially and economically oppressed women should take precedence, since these offer the best hope to undermine patriarchy.

Schüssler Fiorenza stresses the bonds that connect all women; the "option for the most oppressed woman is an option for our women selves."[37] But she has not yet explored in any depth the intermediate tensions between women in an interstructured unjust social order. Because women occupy diverse positions within this unjust social order, there is no necessary correspondence between actions on behalf of more privileged women and those on behalf of the most oppressed woman.

The challenge to give priority to those who are most desperately victimized is a powerful moral challenge. It also presents economically privileged white women with a dilemma. On the one hand, we are called to give priority to the liberation of people other than ourselves—people who suffer an oppression we do not share. On the other hand, a life lived (ostensibly) *for others* is debilitating and frequently covertly manipulative of those others. We cannot really take seriously the oppression of others if we deny ourselves the right to demand that our own exploitation be taken seriously.

White women should demand those conditions that will enable us to grow toward full personhood. There is an honesty and integrity to the process of asserting our own genuine needs. Women who have been socialized to identify with men—to serve men's interests, rather than our own direct interests—need a "theology of self-affirmation."[38] Solid respect for the dignity of others and strong commitment to their welfare is only pos-

---

[35]"Report from the Working Group on Racism/Classism/Sexism," in *Women's Spirit Bonding*, ed. Janet Kalven and Mary I. Buckley (New York: Pilgrim Press, 1984) 132.

[36]Elisabeth Schüssler Fiorenza, "The Will to Choose or to Reject: Continuing Our Critical Work," in *Feminist Interpretation of the Bible*, ed. Letty M. Russell (Philadelphia: Westminster Press, 1985) 127.

[37]Ibid., 128.

[38]Schüssler Fiorenza, *Bread Not Stone*, xv.

sible when it is rooted in affirmation of our own dignity and commitment to our own well-being.

Beverly Harrison has offered a helpful conception of morally legitimate self-assertion. She insists that "self-assertion *is* basic to our moral well-being," but it must be understood in a relational context. Human beings are never isolated, autonomous moral agents. Rather, as persons, we always exist in relationship to other human beings, to nature, and to the divine. Therefore, "all people—each of us-in-relation-to-all—have a mandate, rooted in God, to the sort of self-assertion that grounds and confirms our dignity *in relationship.*"[39]

Human beings are deeply connected to one another. As a result, white women are diminished—perhaps in ways that are not obvious—by the distorted relationships between the races. As the feminists who cooperated in writing *Your Daughters Shall Prophesy* realized, racist social structures have a damaging effect on white women, too, but these consequences are masked by white women's privileges.

> These consequences—a distorted ethnocentric view of the world, a limited understanding of ourselves and our history, a sense of competitiveness that motivates us to stay "on top"; in short, *a lack of freedom and wholeness which results from participating in a system that denies these qualities to others*—are hidden behind the facade of privilege and the myth of cultural superiority.[40]

The most creative moral stance for white women is one in which we are sensitive to our connectedness to all other women and affirm their needs as we assert our own. Such an awareness of connectedness must be based on a realistic appraisal of differences in our experiences. Only an interstructured social analysis can keep our faith in a deep connectedness from degenerating into an ideology that either entraps us in perpetual, debilitating self-sacrifice or legitimates destructive assertion of the immediate interests of our own group.

The Theological Grounds of Human Relationality

One of the strengths of feminist theology is its mandate to examine the divine reality that is the foundation for right human relationships. Exploring the connection between a vision of human wholeness experienced in right relationship and relevant theological descriptions of the divine is very difficult. Constructive feminist theology that explores images and language to communicate our experience of the divine is in its

---

[39] Beverly Wildung Harrison, "Theological Reflection in the Struggle for Liberation: A Feminist Perspective," in *Making the Connections*, ed. Robb, 240-41.

[40] The Cornwall Collective, *Your Daughters Shall Prophesy: Feminist Alternatives in Theological Education* (New York: Pilgrim Press, 1980) 42 (emphasis added).

early stages. As feminists act to enhance the possibilities for right human relationship in the world, we develop new senses of the divine presence in our world. "Out of a moral struggle to embody deeper patterns of human community, freshly empowering visions of God are [being] born."[41]

In a dialectical process, feminist ethicists select images and metaphors for the divine based on the power of these images and metaphors to call forth active commitment to love and justice. As theological ethicists, feminists also draw upon theological images and ideas in order to ground their ethics—to root it firmly in some vision of ultimate reality. We ask which virtues and actions are consistent with our emerging understandings of the divine. At present, those feminist ethicists who are not convinced that "traditional" theological positions are fully adequate to a feminist ethic speak with caution. White feminist theologians who are aware that black women have had few opportunities as theologians to explore rigorously their own experience of the divine will speak with even greater caution.

Nonetheless, divine being, whatever else may be said of it, is the power of right relationship. Beverly Harrison claims that a distinctive human experience of God/ess is the experience of "the presence and power between us when we are reciprocally related to each other in mutual dependence, *and* in the capacity to affect one another." According to Carter Heyward, we know the Power in Relation which is deity in our moments of shared power and reciprocal respect. When we enlarge our personal capacity for reciprocal respect and create institutions that foster mutual power, we co-operate with the divine. For "God is our power in relation to each other, all humanity, and creation itself. God is creative power, that which effects justice—right relation—in history."[42]

There is an interesting convergence between this depiction of God/dess as Power in Relation and some of Mary Daly's imagery. In *Pure Lust* Daly has eloquently invoked "Elemental Participation in Powers of Be-ing." Elemental Be-ing is the source that connects women, all livings things, and the cosmic elements. Daly plays with a rich variety of symbols and metaphors to name reality as it is experienced by women. "Of course, there can be no One Absolutely Right symbol for all Lusty women, for we belong to different tribes and have great individual diversity."[43]

Indeed, there is great diversity among feminist theologians. Daly now rejects Christian symbols for the divine. A number of other white feminist

---

[41]Beverly Wildung Harrison, *Our Right to Choose: Toward a New Ethic of Abortion* (Boston: Beacon Press, 1983) 91.

[42]Beverly Wildung Harrison, "Restoring the Tapestry of Life: The Vocation of Feminist Theology," *The Drew Gateway* 54 (Fall 1983): 45; Isabel Carter Heyward, *The Redemption of God: A Theology of Mutual Relation* (Lanham MD: University Press of America, 1982) 6.

[43]Daly, *Pure Lust,* 25.

theologians, however, find in key biblical images, texts, and themes an expression of God's will that human beings live a full life in right relationship to one another. These theologians often emphasize texts that picture God (or Jesus) as active in behalf of the liberation of the oppressed. Ruether extols the prophetic and messianic tradition of the Bible, which constantly criticizes existing religious and other social institutions in light of the liberating Word of God. God's will stands in judgment on all forms of injustice—of domination by the wealthy and the powerful over a variety of marginalized and despised groups. Ruether emphasizes the prophetic message and praxis of Jesus. Jesus renounces relationships characterized by hierarchical domination and creates new relationships based on service and mutual empowerment.[44]

Schüssler Fiorenza searches for liberating feminist paradigms in the experiences of the earliest Christian communities. She explores the tension between patriarchal social and ecclesiastical structures and "the vision and praxis of the discipleship of equals." The active participation of many women in the Jesus movement and in the missionary communities of the Greco-Roman world, she indicates, emerged out of Jesus' announcement of God's *basileia* (kingdom), which came as good news for the impoverished and other socially marginal persons. Schüssler Fiorenza proposes a feminist historical reconstruction of the experiences of women in biblical times as a subversive memory with the power to propel us toward an inclusive, egalitarian, feminist future.[45]

Some black feminist theologians stress that the liberating Word of God, especially as interpreted by the black church, has had—and continues to have—the power to call black women forth toward freedom. Reviewing the history of black women since Emancipation, Katie Geneva Cannon argues, "It was biblical faith grounded in the prophetic tradition that helped Black women devise strategies and tactics to make Black people less susceptible to the indignities and proscriptions of an oppressive white social order."[46] For many contemporary black women, the Bible continues to be a primary source of liberating vision—particularly in its stories of the Exodus community of liberation and of Jesus the liberator of the oppressed. Feminist ethicists and theologians must continue to search for language and metaphors to name the divine being which empowers relationships of mutual respect between black people and white people.

---

[44]Rosemary Radford Ruether, *Sexism and God-Talk: Toward a Feminist Theology* (Boston: Beacon Press, 1983) 135-38.

[45]Schüssler Fiorenza, "The Will to Choose or to Reject," 134; Elisabeth Schüssler Fiorenza, *In Memory of Her: A Feminist Theological Reconstruction of Christian Origins* (New York: Crossroad Press, 1983).

[46]Katie Geneva Cannon, "The Emergence of Black Feminist Consciousness," in *Feminist Interpretation of the Bible,* ed. Russell, 35.

Communities of Accountability

In order to remain morally responsible, feminists also require communities of accountability in which persons from diverse racial, ethnic, and/or economic backgrounds hold themselves mutually responsible for a struggle to create a just society. Contemporary American society is fragmented along lines of race and class, so few of us have experienced such communities of accountability, and some of them existed for only brief periods of time.[47] We are still learning what the diversity of racial, ethnic, and economic backgrounds means in the lives of other members of our communities. This process of community building is never easy and can be painful, but we must have such communities. For just as the sin of racism manifests itself in both destructive social structures and evil individual attitudes, the process of personal conversion from racism begins with, and must be sustained by, participation in communities struggling toward liberation for all the marginalized.

Over the long term, the communities of accountability that we need must have members of diverse racial, ethnic, and economic groups, since the repeated encounter with another person who demands respect and who calls us to account for ways in which we have oppressed her or him is a powerful prod for moral behavior. Nevertheless, white women in all-white groups do not have to wait or (worse) to import a black woman to be the "visiting expert" before we begin to deal with racism. Since racism is our problem as white women, we can, and should, hold ourselves mutually accountable by making racism an important focus of the activities of white feminist groups.

In order to create communities which do include members of diverse racial, ethnic, and economic groups, we will have to address the cultural and economic barriers which make it unattractive, difficult, or impossible for some women to participate. For example, a recent national meeting of feminists concerned with religious issues met in a big convention hotel. Some of the working-class women found the hotel too large and alienating. The location detracted from their ability to participate in the community. Creating inclusive communities of accountability requires that we assess the needs of diverse participants, reflect the different values of those participants in entertainment and worship events as well as working sessions, and make it economically feasible for everyone to participate.

Feminist communities of accountability will have to struggle constantly with racism. "Only insofar as we face and name and pay respect to our broken places can we even hope to catch glimpses of our body as

---

[47]Some communities of accountability might be local religious groups. However, many feminist communities of accountability do not name themselves explicitly as religious. Moreover, many white religious organizations are not prepared to deal seriously with either sexism or racism.

One."[48] We must understand ourselves as always in the process of acknowledging and correcting the ways in which we fail to do justice.[49] In other words, the communities we need are communities marked by a shared commitment to the long process of developing relationships characterized by mutual respect among persons from diverse races and classes. Such communities require not just personal fidelity to the process of change, but structures that support and require mutual accountability.

In particular, founding and sustaining such communities will mean that middle-class white women will have to pledge ourselves to deal directly with the painful conflict between white and black women that seems inevitable in this racist society. Many middle-class white women have been socialized to avoid conflict, to smooth over troubled feelings, to be "reconcilers."[50] Reconciliation skills are valuable ones, but premature reconciliation does not heal. Rather it covers over wounds that fester. More privileged white women also need to avoid a temptation to withdraw when racial conflicts are painful. As theological ethicist Katie Geneva Cannon warns, white women who feel threatened too often "take their toys, their funds, their programs, their printing press, and go home, where they can perch on a ledge and not have their boat rocked. This in itself is privilege."[51] In a racist society, privileged white women can withdraw to enclaves where there is no *overt* racial conflict.

While many white women need fortitude to struggle with racial conflict instead of withdrawing or striving for premature reconciliation, other white and black women must avoid *destructive* charges of racism—those that do not stimulate positive change, but rather dehumanize and (often) paralyze the accused. The processes through which racism within the feminist movement is addressed are important. Discussions of racism can degenerate into "trashing" sessions in which the victims are assaulted for their racist attitudes and practices by others who assume the dominant role as possessors of "superior moral sensitivities."

When feminist groups discuss racism they can be immobilized in the quicksand of anger and guilt. White women need to be especially careful

[48]The Mudflower Collective, *God's Fierce Whimsy*, 63.

[49]Schüssler Fiorenza, *Bread Not Stone*, 7. See also Rosemary Radford Ruether, "Envisioning Our Hopes: Some Models of the Future," in *Women's Spirit Bonding*, ed. Kalven and Buckley, 334-35.

[50]This comment is based upon discussions at the Feminist Theory Group, Bunting Institute, Spring 1985, and comments in The Mudflower Collective, *God's Fierce Whimsy*, 94-99. See also Audre Lorde, "The Uses of Anger: Women Responding to Racism," in *Sister Outsider: Essays and Speeches* (Trumansburg NY: Crossing Press, 1984) 131.

[51]The Mudflower Collective, *God's Fierce Whimsy*, 39.

that our guilt does not become another excuse for inaction when racial issues are at stake. As Adrienne Rich warns,

> guilt feelings—so easily provoked in women that they have become almost a form of social control—can also become . . . a preoccupation with our own feelings which prevents us from ever connecting with the experience of others. Guilt feelings paralyze, but paralysis can become a convenient means of remaining passive and instrumental. If I cannot even approach you because I feel so much guilt towards you, I need never listen to what you actually have to say; I need never risk making common cause with you.[52]

White and black feminists need to create empowering alternative modes of conversation and action—ones which mutually strengthen us for the struggle against sexism and racism. As black feminist Audre Lorde acknowledges, "it is very difficult to stand still and to listen to another woman's voice delineate an agony I do not share, or one to which I myself have contributed."[53] Such listening is a critical task for members of communities of accountability.

Feminist religious communities struggling toward full human liberation need religious rituals in which we confess our sins and embody our moments of reconciliation. Moments of honest confession of the evil—individual and corporate—we have done can propel us into action to change our evil attitudes and to transform evil structures. As Carter Heyward states, "Our passion drives us into our confession which is always our first just act."[54] Those of us who are white feminists need to voice our confession of the sin of racism and pledge ourselves to personal and social repentance with poetry, music, and movement. White and black persons need ceremonies to embody our commitments to mutual respect.[55]

We need to explore our differences in dialogue and in action, not only because some of our differences divide us and drain energy away from the struggle to transform society, but also because our differences can be enriching and empowering. Those of us who are white need to learn about the distinctive skills black women have developed—skills that can strength-

---

[52]Adrienne Rich, "Disloyal to Civilization: Feminism, Racism, and Gynephobia," in *On Lies, Secrets, and Silences: Selected Prose, 1966-1978* (New York: W. W. Norton and Company, 1979) 306-307.

[53]Audre Lorde, "The Uses of Anger," in *Sister Outsider,* 128.

[54]Heyward, *The Redemption of God,* 161.

[55]Examples of such feminist rituals which explore racism and redemption from racism have been created by members of the Women's Alliance for Theology, Ethics, and Ritual, a feminist group that develops resources for social change and community building. The address is WATER, 8035 13th Street, Silver Spring MD 20910.

en the women's movement as a whole. For example, many black women
assess more realistically the resistance powerful persons will exert in order
to thwart change and to maintain the status quo. Since most black women
have felt the full force of racism from early childhood, they understand
well the intransigence of unjust social institutions. On the other hand, those
white women who have intimate access to men with power often naively
overestimate our influence. Privileged white women could learn some astute judgment from our black sisters.

Enriching and empowering differences can be a continuing source of
strength in the liberation struggle. However, in striving to appreciate creative differences, white women must not replace more negative stereotypes of black women with a romantic caricature of the strong, nurturing,
black mammy who will carry us all to freedom. Stereotypes do not accu-
rately name any woman's strengths.

Fidelity to relationships of mutual respect is something white women
will have to manifest anew each day. It is not one's past conduct toward
black people alone that matters. The question will always be "how one
stands today." Black women, who have been betrayed so frequently by
white women, will continue to look for actions from us that confirm that
we can be trusted.[56]

A feminist theology adequate to the struggle for the liberation of *all*
women—and ultimately *all* persons—will have to be rooted in diverse human experiences. In particular feminist theology requires that we all seek
out and appreciate that which is positive and powerful in black women's
experience.

Conclusion

White feminists must keep alive painful historical memories of the
racism that disfigures our past as white persons and as white feminists. We
must reject any renewed version of the True Womanhood myth that obscures our involvement in the sins of racism both individually and insti-
tutionally. Any self-deceptive overconfidence in our own moral strength
will undermine our contributions to the struggle for the liberation of all
women.

We need to continue probing the interstructuring of racism and sexism. We must be cautious about any oversimplified model of social
oppression that makes the evil we white women know best—sexism—the
taproot of all other social evils. A more nearly adequate social analysis of

---

[56]The Mudflower Collective, *God's Fierce Whimsy*, 40. The phrase "how one
stands today" is found in a letter from a black women's leader, Ellen C. Carter, to
white suffragist Ida Husted Harper. The incident is described in Paula Giddings,
When and Where I Enter: The Impact of Black Women on Race and Sex in America (New
York: William Morrow and Company, 1984) 161-62.

the roots of human oppressions also requires attention to the interconnections between racism and sexism and forms of prejudice and domination based on age, physical or mental abilities, or sexual preference. Further investigation of the interlinking of sexism, racism, and economic exploitation is especially urgent.

In a society where sexism, racism, and economic exploitation are interstructured, the assertion of morally legitimate group interest by white women—especially economically privileged white women—requires careful and creative moral judgment. White women should neither perpetually set aside our own demands for the sake of supporting "the most oppressed woman" nor pursue group interest while remaining culpably naive about destructive, dehumanizing effects of our actions on others. We need to develop conceptions of self and group interest which recognize that our own freedom and wholeness is diminished when we willingly participate in social relationships that deny those qualities to others.

Feminist theologians are called to envision religious institutions, ideas, and images that will enhance the possibilities for right human relationship. In order to conjure up powerful theological images we need to be particularly attentive to the visions and voices of black women. Communities of accountability are the locations where we can hear each other's dreams and share each other's visions. Communities of accountability give us an opportunity to draw upon each other's strengths.

It is in communities of accountability that we will be called to continuing repentance for our ongoing involvement in racism. Such communities are also important locations in which we experience that grace which empowers us to develop new relationships between white and black persons—relationships characterized by justice and mutual respect. Grace strengthens white women with fortitude to face the long, difficult process of transforming prejudiced personal attitudes and behaviors and unjust social institutions.

Today, experiences of genuine community among white and black people are rare, fragmentary, and tenuous. Our unity is imperiled by the legacy of suspicion and distrust from our past, the distortions caused by contemporary racist cultural values and social institutions, and white passivity in the face of racial injustice. However, commitment to justice for all women in our concrete, interstructured situations of oppression motivates us to struggle toward more just relationships and social structures. In the struggle to obtain justice for ourselves and for all persons, we experience greater unity and begin to sense more compellingly the wholeness that is personal dignity realized in right relation.

Index

DATE DUE